MAKE YOUR DREAMS COME TRUE NOW!

How to Manifest Your Wishes, Dreams and Desires

CATHERINE ATHANS, PH.D.

ANGELS ISLAND PRESS
LOS ALTOS, CA

Angels Island Press
An Angels Island Production
303 First Street, Suites 1 & 2
Los Altos, CA 94022
www.angelsislandpress.com
1-888-58ANGEL

Portions of the proceeds from the sale of this book go to benefit the MORGAN MANOR FOUNDATION®—a charitable organization which provides grassroots support and education to single parent families. THE MORGAN MANOR FOUNDATION® is a project of the National Heritage Foundation®.

For more information please visit http://www.morganmanorfoundation.org

Library of Congress Control Number: 2007926218

ISBN 10: 0-9794380-0-4
ISBN 13: 978-0-9794380-0-4

Book Design by Dotti Albertine: www.albertinebookdesign.com
Illustrations by Frank Barcenas: www.frankbarcenas.com
Cover Photo by Getty Images

ABOUT MORGAN MANOR

Morgan Manor—Foundation: A project of the National Heritage Foundation

Part of the impetus for writing this book was to give support to my charitable foundation, Morgan Manor.

The inspiration for **Morgan Manor,** which I founded, came from A. S. Neil's Summer Hill, *A New View of Childhood*—a book that discusses freedom and democracy in education. I read this book in my late teens, and was struck by the themes of freedom for children —giving back humanity to people who have lost it.

With these thoughts in hand, from the age of eighteen, I dreamed of a special school for children. I wondered if it were possible for a school to exist that allowed children to express their potential, instead of the stifling lessons given by modern education—to create a school where children are treated as the special beings of God that they are—with love, care, and attention. Since then, I've been seeking a new paradigm in education that supports both children and parents spiritually, mentally, emotionally, and physically.

Morgan Manor's role is to make a better quality of life more accessible to families, single parents, women, and children. If everyone is doing well, then it will create a better community.

—CATHERINE ATHANS, PH.D.

For information on sponsorships, donating funds, services, volunteering, and more, please call, write or visit the Morgan Manor Foundation website.

www.morganmanorfoundation.org
303 First Street, Los Altos, California USA 94022
650.948.1796

Dedication

I dedicate this book to my wonderful clients,
loyal friends, and nourishing family.

Your courage is inspirational!

Your journey of transformation wonderful!

I thank you, one and all, for all the magic
you bring into this world.

CONTENTS

Preface

I WANT TO LET YOU ALL KNOW—

It took me many years to realize the significance of how many lies were told as *Truths* and the kind of damage these *untruths* cause for a lifetime.

I had begun to realize while in college that untruths were foisted upon us by our well meaning friends, families, churches, synagogues, temples, schools, and society.

Make Your Dreams Come True Now was conceived many years ago when I created a workshop called, "Letting Go the Lie."

Lies form an energy pattern in the body, mind and spirit that permeates the Divine Pattern to form a sabotage mechanism in the system.

Getting to Truth requires recognizing these untruths and dissolving them—a simple concept but a very difficult task.

This book is a compilation of many, many years of hard work, study, lessons and spiritual cleansings; and mostly an impassioned desire to know Truth to set us free!

In this book I have presented what I have learned in a concise, easy-to-read format that really works.

I pray that you receive the infinite blessings that are opening for you as you read and do the work on the following pages.

Note From the Author

EVEN AS A YOUNG CHILD, I had a desire to know the Truth—the highest levels of Truth. I looked for Truth from all teachings, and I set out on a quest to learn from as many different perspectives as possible.

My deep desire to know Truth, to find Truth, has led me to the deepest places in my soul and sometimes the greatest darkness of my being. It has led me to the greatest heights and ushered me into amazing realms and dimensions which have revealed their wondrous secrets. It has showed me infinite possibilities and opened my willingness to know beyond what words might express. Through these journeys I have learned to have a deep compassion and respect for the human spirit.

My quest has led me to study and be with those who practice a deep seeking and teaching, from seekers of wisdom to professors of science; from world leaders to tribal chiefs; from kahunas to professors of medicine and the clergy everywhere.

Part of my reason for sharing my understanding and my journey with you is to give you a means to enter this path of self-discovery in a step-by-step proven manner. As I gained the knowledge, recognized the Truths and allowed the Truths to be active in my life, the Truths then unleashed great joy, love, and prosperity.

Through my therapeutic and private healing practices, I have been privileged to travel with my clients to new, unexplored realms of reality where a new world view for the client emerges. My clients gain a new idea of who and what they are. It is a marvelous dance full of wonder and magic!

As I see my clients grow to lead the lives that they were born to lead, putting into practice the Truths and principles presented in this book, I am compelled to make the same available to all who wish to seek.

The principles in this book are the principles and practices that are a daily ritual for me. Daily, I live in love, praise, gratitude, and appreciation, remembering to give thanks for the blessings which flow to me and from me.

Daily, I acknowledge the blessings which have manifested in my life, a life that is rich in health and happiness.

Daily, I give thanks for my family, my wonderful clients, my warm home and terrific supportive friends.

I am honored to be a part of my clients' healing, evolution, and growth.

I am humbled by their strength and courage!

—CATHERINE ATHANS, PH.D.

*This Book is Written
to Assist You in Changing Your Life*

All my love,
Catherine

Section One

INTRODUCTION

THERE IS AN ANCIENT STORY about guarding the secrets of the universe. It was said that the elders, the wise ones of the world, got together to see how they could protect the secrets of the universe. One wise one suggested placing the secrets in a sealed box and hiding them under the sea. But several responded "no" because man is curious and will go under the sea. Then one said, "Hide the secrets on top of a mountain," but several responded "no" because man needs challenge and will be challenged to conquer the mountain. Then, from the back of the crowd, an old woman spoke up and said the only place to hide the secrets of the universe is inside the Self because man will never seek to look there. At the old woman's suggestion, there was silent agreement. Today you may find all the secrets of the universe hidden neatly inside of you waiting for your personal journey of discovery and delight.

Knowing the Truth will allow you to begin to know reality: God the Source. In knowing God, marvelous things happen. You begin to know your Self and others. You have more compassion. You are able to both develop kindness in your heart and practice kindness in your daily life. You can see more easily what is good for you and what is not. Life begins to get easier because you become more clear and less confused. Life takes on many different and interesting facets. Life becomes more fun each day.

Searching for the Truth is not easy. It is fraught with danger. Like Indiana Jones, we need to overcome creatures and recognize the booby traps to step around, over, or through to the chest of golden valuables —the Truth and Truths of your heart, the Love and great sense of Grace that is waiting for you.

The great treasures lie deeply buried within your heart—your boundless love is connecting you to the universe and to unlimited abundance.

This is the journey on which every student must go.

The great secrets are right there with you. No matter how ordinary you may feel, you are *NOT*.

YOU ARE SO MUCH MORE ### *SO VERY MUCH MORE.*

When Socrates said, "Know thyself," he was not asking you for a casual acquaintance. He was asking for a lifelong dedicated study. It is through this self-knowledge that all of the secrets of the universe are revealed. It is through knowing the Self that God is revealed.

Your quest becomes the Great Adventure—*your great adventure*. Please know that you are never alone—*ever*—your wonderful angels and guidance are helping you and waiting for YOUR CALL.

This book will teach you how to:

- Let go the lies—distinguish fact from fiction

- Dissolve those bindings that have been binding or paralyzing you and keeping you from the richness that you were born into as your divine right

- Get back on the path to love

- Benefit from great teachers' principles

- Learn universal principles that operate just under the surface of life

- Open the channels to abundance, to receive and rejoice in abundance

- Grow in your family relationships and have more satisfying social relationships

- Live a life that is filled with fulfillment, health, joy, delight and love

- Find the healing power in your words

- Re-establish hope for your life

- Connect with the Universal Source and your Divine pattern

- Gain the life that God—the Source—has for you

- Live the life that you were born to live

- Make your life work

  – Be well.
  – Have fun.
  – Enjoy!

Your Divine Right

As unique beings of light, each of us has our own wishes, dreams, and desires which, when fulfilled, bring to our lives a great sense of well-being, peace, and happiness.

Develop a Positive Attitude and Discover the Power Within by:

- **Activating Your Imagination**

- **Developing the Skill of Discernment**

- **Living in Love, Praise, Gratitude, and Appreciation**

- **Manifesting Your Wishes, Dreams, and Desires**

Make Your Dreams Come True Now!

This is a four-part series of lessons designed to support you in your journey to be master of yourself and to create in your life what your heart knows will bring you GREAT JOY.

The first lesson—*ACTIVATING YOUR IMAGINATION*—offers an explanation of the imagination. This lesson emphasizes that we all need to open to our imagination and nourish it. The imagination, when active, actually opens *new channels* of energy allowing you to grow. In addition, it opens you to *new facets* of God, expanding your reality to make living a much more interesting and fulfilling experience. This first lesson will awaken in you the *possibilities* that you wish to appear in your life. You will start to envision the MAGIC within. You will be provided certain tools and practices that will support you in activating your imagination.

The second lesson—*DEVELOPING THE SKILL OF DISCERN-MENT*—will help you to develop an inner guidance system that will assist you in "knowing" what is true for you. It will also help you to develop an *inner compass* and *access your powers* of intuition. The techniques, tools, and information in this second lesson will help you develop the skill of discernment, a skill you will use in all aspects of your life.

The third lesson—*LIVING IN LOVE, PRAISE, GRATITUDE, AND APPRECIATION (LPGA)*—will help you see the blessings which are in your life *right now.* You will learn how to get the magic flowing and *honor new blessings* as they appear. A new clarity in love, praise, gratitude, and appreciation will help you to pursue those possibilities that are right for you. In addition, the third lesson will continue to facilitate *opening new channels* of opportunity and cleaning any stuck channels, where the flow is sporadic. Further it will help you to develop your faith in your desires, so that you can begin to *rely* on *fulfillment* as a *regular* part of your life.

The fourth lesson—*MANIFESTING YOUR WISHES, DREAMS, AND DESIRES*—brings together the elements of "making things so" in the three-dimensional world and everyday life. You will learn how action is required to bring about what you are seeking and how the interaction of you, the elements of manifestation, and the abundance of the Source that surrounds you—all become a *wondrous, magical,* and *delightful dance*—one of great love and *many blessings.*

You will learn how to take your intuitive leads into your everyday life to make them "real." You will then bring them into existence in the three-dimensional realm. What had been an idea, inspiration or intuition is now a part of life that you experience through your five senses.

The Importance of Affirmations, Meditations and Guided Imagery

To assist you with your personal journey, at the end of each lesson are *affirmations, meditations*, and *guided imagery* which flow from the principles presented in the lesson. Each of these activities is vital to changing your life. Please take time to use these tools in each lesson to receive the most from the teachings.

AFFIRMATIONS are tremendous tools in effecting change in your life, for as you state your affirmations aloud and with feeling, you are providing guidance to your spirit to go forth into the energy Source and bring from God, our Source, what your words are affirming.

Affirmations are always stated in the present tense and with positive statements using the *I Am* form, because you want a focal point in the universe. *I Am* is God as God made you. Using the present tense, *I Am*, you are telling the universe, through God, to make it so.

Because our Source has no time line, our subconscious mind works in the PRESENT TENSE, and because in Truth, past and future don't exist, it is the NOW which exists.

I am NOW completely prepared and fully equipped to meet what is mine today.

I am NOW willing to receive that which is to my highest good.

MEDITATION is another tool which you may need to affect change in your life. The meditations provided will help you get back in touch with your *self*, your Source, your DIVINE pattern, your unique vibration, your own unique being.

MEDITATION

QUIETS THE NOISE

IN YOUR MIND,

ALLOWING YOU

TO FOCUS.

Meditation allows for a *re-acquaintance*
on a deeper level of your *self* and facilitates
harmony between your inner being and the Source,
bringing your focus to the God within.

IF YOU ARE NEW TO MEDITATION, let me suggest that you meditate at the same time each day. At first limit yourself to three minutes per meditation. You will soon realize that meditation can be a wonderful start to your day.

Meditation is a way to attune the
SELF, *heart, mind and soul.*

In meditation your INNER SELF is acknowledged.

In your daily life you spend much of your time dealing with the outer world, the world that you allow to dictate who you are and what you can have.

In the practice of meditation
you are able to let go of the outer circumstances,
and you are able to tune in and sense things
that you don't normally perceive.

Meditating—prior to stating your affirmations—allows your body, spirit, and mind to slow down and become calm. Then your affirmations and intentions go forth into the universe with *greater ease* and *more intensity.*

The Importance of Journaling

To further assist you in your personal journey, at the end of each lesson are journal pages which you may use to write down your feelings, thoughts, and ideas.

Journaling...
is an important instrument of growth,
as the act of writing involves more nerve endings
(from hand to brain) than any other activity
you do during your daily routine.

When you write, you are transmuting a concept, a feeling, an inkling into words as symbols and then linking those symbols together to create a whole concept or mood which then touches the self in a new and different way.

When you write...
you are cementing symbols into the brain.

Your brain is *perceiving* as it is creating.

Writing down or journaling opens the channels for more inspiration to come to you.

Writing is a quiet activity, as is meditation.

Glimmers of intuition often appear during the journaling process.

*This inspiration, once received,
is woven into new behaviors and feelings.*

When you journal, please just write what comes to you—a word, a phrase. Don't worry about grammar, just allow what is inside of you to spring forth onto the page.

Just enjoy...

How to Use This Book

This book is a beginning basic text in *METAPHYSICAL LAW*, the laws of living. It is intended that you read each chapter in order and that you work through the exercises which are designed to help you put into practice the principles of each lesson.

You may choose to read each chapter more than once and underline those passages which resonate with you.

Remember...
that as you are a unique individual,
your journey is also unique.

Allow yourself to establish a rhythm, a beat. Allow yourself to go with your rhythm and experience yourself differently from the self that is often presented to the world.

It is vital when you start on a path of change that you have a *willingness* for things in your life to be *different*. This may seem a rather simple statement...

...take a moment right now and think about this.

Please know that by reading this book and actively putting into practice the lessons, you are *beginning* to *access* tremendous *hidden faculties*.

YOU ARE BEGINNING
A JOURNEY TO THE SELF
—A JOURNEY OF
TRUTH AND WISDOM.

This is the journey which leads you
back to your TRUE SELF
and thus to GOD—the SOURCE within.

You become interested in who you are and what you are. You become more interested in the life that is there all around you!

When these lessons are activated in your everyday life, they will bring you joy, richness, fullness, and happiness.

Consider the knowledge—that will be gained through both exploration and information in each lesson—to be a CORNERSTONE UPON WHICH YOU MAY BUILD.

As you progress through this book, and through your life, always come back to the SOURCE within you, the GOD within. Seek those quiet answers using the tools revealed in each chapter.

Please remember that through the words, tools, and concepts in this book, there is GREAT LOVE FOR YOU.

Know that there is great support for you to fulfill your *DIVINE DESTINY* in the angelic realms.

Call on your angels often!

Growth is exciting and energizing.

Life will be rich.

Each day will be a magnificent adventure awaiting you and awaiting the wishes you have to be fulfilled.

Credence, love, acceptance and compassion to you during this, your journey—I now share with you these Truths...

Be well and have fun.

ACTIVATE YOUR IMAGINATION

First It Must Be Imagined...

IMAGINATION is the act or power of forming mental images of what may not be actually present or what may not have actually been experienced.

Imagination is more than a faculty of the mind ...

Imagination is a flowing, intuitive gift.

Imagination is the ability to see what could be.

Imagination is bringing into being—from little or nothing—great richness.

Imagination is the first tool that one needs
to manifest, to create, what will be.

This lesson, *ACTIVATING YOUR IMAGINATION,* teaches you to create a multi-faceted, in-depth, rich experience of your senses.

You will mentally create a reality which will bring you joy, happiness, and a full life.

*The process of imagining provides you
with an avenue to a richer participation in your own life,
for it is your imagination, your thoughts,
which create your perceptions of the world in which you live.*

Think of this. *You are the one perceiving your world.* Because of this you are the one who may CHANGE YOUR PERCEPTION.

Imagination is a key in doing this.

Taking the time to activate your imagination is key to obtaining what will bring you to your highest good.

Please take a moment and consider the following ...

Nothing exists today that wasn't first imagined!

To invent,
to dream,
to create,
and to design
require first
the activation
of your
imagination.

Take a moment right now and think about the last time you met a person who was full of life, energy and vigor. I share with you that you were in the company of someone with an active imagination who did not rely solely on outside stimuli to give interest to life.

To be a person with an active imagination is to be in touch with what you really are inside your heart.

Allow your heart feelings, inklings
and ideas to take shape and form.

Perhaps you imagine in pictures or sensations...

...Maybe you imagine the words you would like to speak or hear spoken to you.

...Maybe you see yourself as relaxed and calm.

...Maybe you imagine yourself as completely confident.

...Maybe you know what you do is very positive and will bring the best result for everyone concerned, including yourself.

Please know that
your rich imagination
is the beginning
of your amazing
transformation!

For those of you thinking, "Catherine, I wouldn't know where to start," I ask you to go back to memories of your childhood.

Do you remember the games you used to play?

Do you remember playing *dress-up* and *pretend*?

As a child, much of your daily play started in your *IMAGINATION*.

It was your *IMAGINATION* that allowed you to put on a few articles of clothing and become for that moment someone other than your four- or five-year-old self.

It was your *IMAGINATION* that allowed you to put on a cowboy hat and grab a stick or broom and go *ride the range* looking for buffalo and bandits.

It was your *IMAGINATION* that turned that large cardboard box into a *racing car* zooming through the turns of the Indianapolis 500 speed-way.

Be As A Child

CHILDREN'S USE OF IMAGINATION IS SATISFYING, NOUR-ISHING, FUN, AND NATURAL. It was through your childhood imagination that you first envisioned yourself as an adult.

It was in your childhood imagination that you first began to rehearse and embellish the dreams you had for being a grown-up.

Did you imagine yourself as a police officer?

Or were you a princess or a fireman?

Did you have dreams about being a cowboy or a dancer?

Did you look up into the sky
and think about piloting an airplane?

Did you see a truck go by and imagine yourself as the driver taking your haul down the long highway? How much fun you had making the truck horn sound again and again!

Or perhaps, you thought about when you would be a mommy or a daddy with children of your own.

It was in the active
imagination of your childhood
that your life's dreams, wishes,
and desires were first born.

Can you remember what your dreams were for yourself when you were a young child or a teenager?

Are you now living those dreams?

If not, what happened to your dreams?

Do you remember changing?

Perhaps the change began when you started to attend school.

Older kids may have put you down, calling you a *baby* because you were able to entertain yourself with just your wonderful faculty of imagination.

The Evaporation of Imagination

In school, flights of fancy were no longer regarded as adorable and wonderful but rather were to be *curbed* and *contained*. School time was allocated to filling your brain with facts reproducible on standardized tests.

The creative, unfettered, imagination so much a part of childhood play began to be *left behind*.

The value of a *creative* and *active* imagination, which is not easily quantifiable, became of less importance.

More time was spent on learning and giving the right answer. It should come as no surprise that for many people...

...the vivid wonders of childhood imagination trickled away.

Imagination Replaced By A Stark World

Sometimes people find that their childhood world of wonder and delight has been replaced by a stark world of adult responsibilities governed solely by reason, rules and logic. Time as an adult is not spent in enjoying an active imagination and dreaming dreams but rather in staying rigidly on a path of duty.

Pleasure is bridled or eliminated in favor of practicality. Life becomes much less than it could be. As your imagination is diminished in use, so too are your expectations for what you sought to achieve in your life.

What did you give up?

- Did you give up your heart's desire for what Mom or Dad wanted you to do?

- Did you change your major in school to one where you were told you would get a good job?

- Did your view of the world as wondrous change to a view of the world that was suspect and not to be trusted, but manipulated, because you were told and believed that your heart's desire wasn't practical?

> *As a result, did you begin*
> *to distrust your feelings*
> *and trade them in for*
> *some system outside yourself?*

The gradual slowdown
in the use of your imagination
dissolved a part of your being.
It may have left you feeling helpless.

Failing to use or develop
the imagining faculty
interferes with *self-esteem.*

It may leave you feeling too ashamed
to develop a vivid imagination.

It can be devastating.

What You Can Do

Did you know that it is in activating and using your imagination that you—your life force, your core, your very essence—become LARGER than when you dwelt in the world of rules and logic?

Unfortunately, the inverse is also true.

Not using your imagination leads to a diminishing of the very life force within.

Think back—were there times that you settled for what you had out of fear?

Did you settle for fear of scarcity?

Did you not allow yourself to dream of more?

Did you not allow yourself to

dream BIG?

You Are Alive!

YOU ARE ALIVE. If you are reading this book there is part of you that is pursuing your fulfillment—and part of that is re-igniting your imagining faculty.

YOU CAN CHANGE.

Having an active imagination is the first step to having the life you desire.

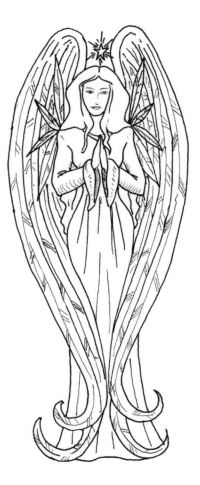

Imagination—Like A Genie In A Bottle

Take time now to ponder and picture this—

> *Your imagination is like a genie in a bottle*
> *that has been corked up for years.*

Reading this book and doing the accompanying exercises is a solid first step to uncorking the bottle and letting the magic genie out.

And unlike the traditional genie who only offers three wishes, the wishes, dreams, and desires revealed through your imagination are...

...boundless

...and limitless.

Activating Your Imagination

I understand that going inside and activating your imagination to search for your life's possibilities and opportunities may be uncomfortable or even a bit scary at first.

Using time for purposeful *imagining* may even go against what you have been taught. Perhaps, as you first start to reawaken your imagination, you might remember teachers instructing you to, "Stop daydreaming! You're wasting time!"

Old conditioning has taught that if something is not *productive,* if you don't have something immediately to show for it, you are not using your time wisely...

> *...Now remember a time when you were*
> *acknowledged for your vibrant imagination.*

Go back to when Mom, Dad, Grandma or other adults thought you were the *cutest* and the *best* when you were acting out a desire of your heart.

> *Picture the love that was in their eyes and on their faces.*

GIVE THAT UNCONDITIONAL LOVE TO YOURSELF as you once again start to practice imagination on a regular basis.

What Imagination Can Accomplish

You may know the story of Olympic Gold medalist, Jim Thorpe: *He practiced his broad jumps by lying in a hammock closing his eyes and visualizing the distance that he wanted to jump,* and then visualized himself in every frame, every motion of the jump until he saw himself completing each jump.

As Jim lay in his hammock day after day, his coach became concerned and began to voice his concerns rather loudly. Jim's coach wanted to see Jim practicing and working out. One day, as Jim lay in his hammock with his eyes closed, Jim's coach came over to talk to him. Jim opened his eyes and told his coach he was glad to see him and asked the coach if he would be so kind as to step back another ten feet from the hammock.

Jim's coach was delighted to comply as he thought Jim was going to leap out of the hammock and finally get to work. Instead, Jim looked at the coach, then closed his eyes and gently resumed swinging in the hammock.

The coach became upset and yelled, "Jim, when are you going to start practicing?"

Jim opened one eye and responded,

"Coach, I already am."

What Jim knew was that by using his imagination, through focused visualization, he was *practicing*.

He was practicing on a different level, a different dimensional level.

He was commanding each part of himself through his imagination and establishing in his subconscious mind the outcome he desired: how he would move, what he would feel, and visualizing accepting his medal.

Jim's practicing both in the physical and in his imagination
resulted in his winning the Olympic Gold!

When you become willing
to use your imagination and all your senses,
and become willing to
DREAM A LARGE DREAM,
you begin to manifest your true desires
on the most elementary but necessary level.

This will lead you to attain what you desire,
which brings you to your highest good.

Imagination Gives You Choice

It is your imagination that brings you CHOICE, choices for the life you live and the way you live it.

Take a moment here to stop and think about your choices. Jot these down in your journal.

How did you come to make the choices
you made about life in general? Career? Family?

Were your choices governed by logic, reason, or fear?
Was your intuition or heart's desire involved?

When I speak to you about your heart's desire, how do you feel?

Please consider that your heart holds the keys
to unlock the doors to your great
HAPPINESS, SATISFACTION, and JOY.

Imagination Needs Exercise

It is in using your imagination that channels of joy and delight are created. Think about this a few moments. This concept has not been taught in school. Let me say this again.

It is in using your imagination
that channels of joy and delight are created.

One of the reasons I wrote this book is to help you understand the importance of having an active imagination...

...*to allow your imagination to bring you back to TRUTH.*

Using your imagination is vital to your *very* existence, for it is in using your imagination that you achieve levels of *inspiration* previously unknown.

Inspiration literally means to INFUSE WITH LIFE.

Through using your imagination
you literally make more room for "life" in you.

As you practice activating your imagination, your perception of the physical world will broaden. The limits that time and life may have placed upon your imagination will begin to fall away.

You will find that all your senses and your ability to *vision and imagine* will become much more robust.

> *It is from this newly robust and active imagination that abundance will be created.*

Using your imagination is essential to achieving a personal reality that is rich, lush, fulfilling, and satisfying.

Having an active imagination is key to enriching your life, rediscovering your creativity, and finding a new zest for life.

> *An active imagination is also key to exploring and developing new opportunities and possibilities in all areas of your life.*

The Lock Is Rusty

Perhaps you are now thinking, "Catherine, my lock is rusty, my keys don't seem to work. When I try to go into my imagination I become distracted by the thoughts of what I should be doing such as mowing the lawn or doing the dishes, or I start thinking about what happened at work."

Perhaps for some of you, when you first go to use your imagination, you find you come up blank. How do you get past this?

A simple way is to begin by thinking of your favorite television character or your favorite character from a book. Choose someone who has qualities that you admire and would want to have as your own.

Now *imagine* that character as yourself. Go first for the general picture. Picture yourself wearing the same or similar clothes as your chosen character. Note the shoes and accessories that you are wearing. Continue to fill in your mind's picture.

- Put yourself in a particular setting.
- Are you outside or inside?
- Are there people around you or are you alone?

Now go further: Think about what you would order when choosing a meal. Think about how, as this character, you would interact with others. This is when the magic begins to happen...

Imagine yourself TODAY, in rich detail, doing those things that you want to draw into your life. Then do what you can TODAY to take you a step closer to those changes.

Your action works as a prayer or statement which comes to affirm these attributes as part of you.

**Even if at first it doesn't seem real,
ACT AS IF IT IS.**

Act as You Wish to Be

Socrates stated, *Act as you wish to be,* for to act is to bring it into being; and the first step to acting *as you wish to be* is activating your imagination. For so many of us, we lament the position in which we find ourselves. We wish someone else to move us. We negate the power within that is the *only* real guide that will tell us the *Truth* for our life.

So let go of the outside; practice coming inside.

Let your imagination run wild.
Be an adventurer of your own soul.
Be willing to see what you really are.

Writer Florence Scovell Shin stated, *Whatever man feels deeply or images clearly, is impressed upon the subconscious mind, and carried out in the minutest detail.*

Allow your imagination to carry out
your heart's wishes, dreams, and desires.

Imagination as a Precious Gift

You may use your imagination to alter your mood, your responses to what is going on around you, your daily interactions, your inner feelings, and physical manifestations which flow from above.

> *Think of your imagination as a precious gift,*
> *for an active imagination can have*
> *a profound effect on both your mind and body.*

An active imagination has such a force in and on your life it can be used for much broader healing. Research has shown that activating a person's imagination assists in the healing and treatment of various physical, mental, and emotional illnesses including heart disease, hypertension, post-traumatic stress disorder, and arterial sclerosis.

As Florence Scovell Shin also shares, *What man images, sooner or later, externalizes in his affairs.* She goes on further to explain, "I know of a man who feared a certain disease. It was a very rare disease and difficult to get, but he pictured it continually and read about it until it manifested in his body, and he died, the victim of *distorted imagination.*"

> *Use your imagination to heal.*

Imagination in the Mind-Body Relationship

The Simingtons of Texas (husband and wife physician team) developed a creative visualization process for terminal cancer patients to use to fight and prevail against that dreaded disease.

Medical knowledge affirms the existence of an intimate relationship between mind and body. Doctors and scientists know the power of an active imagination.

An activated imagination can reduce stress and help with healing.

Western medicine now utilizes guided imagery and meditation to assist in activating a person's imagination. Doctors have their cancer patients picture the tumors being blasted by white light.

It is now more common for physicians to prescribe, along with pharmacology, a daily practice of visualization for the healing of the cells and tissues.

Hospitals and clinics around the world now offer classes on the use of imagination and visualization as part of healing and wellness programs.

An activated imagination is used to create or manifest physical changes in both mind and body, including the creation of new neural pathways in the brain and changes in the molecular structure of the cell.

An activated imagination can also
create openings and shift energy
which results in visible, measurable changes.

Through your focused thoughts and intentions,
YOU CAN ALTER MATTER.

There is a story that was in the news many years ago when I was a child. It was about a plane that went down in the Arctic. It took authorities many days to locate the plane, and when they did, they were extremely surprised to find many healthy, vibrant survivors. When the survivors were questioned about how it was they seemed to look robust having no food and being many days in the Arctic, they explained that a group of them decided that the *only way they were going to survive* the cold with no food was to *MAKE BELIEVE* that they lived in a warm and bountiful environment where they were able to choose anything they wanted to eat.

They planned in detail three meals a day, made sure to serve those meals appropriately, sat down and had those meals together, remarking about the goodness of the various fruits, vegetables, and meats they were served. They made sure to tell each other not to overeat because there was plenty for each day. They even went so far as to remark about the nutrition in the various things that they ate, and how it would nourish and support all their bodily systems.

Because of this *ACTIVE USE OF THEIR IMAGINATIONS*, they were able to forego serious illness and even death because their bodies responded as if they indeed were eating the foods that they served, which were totally made out of different patterns of ice!

Take A Different Path

Right now you have the ability, through your imagination, to choose how you will respond. For example, perhaps you and your employer interact in ways that leave you feeling stressed. Or perhaps certain exchanges between you and a friend, your partner, your child, or your parent leave you feeling powerless, weak, or dissatisfied. You want to experience encounters which result in different outcomes.

Use your imagination
to paint a different picture,
to write a different script,
to change your position,
to transmute your feelings.

Through your imagination, picture in your mind what it is that you want in your life.

Allow the ideal situation to form pictures in your mind and place yourself in those pictures.

Give them texture and color.

This is the starting point for change.

It may take a little time for the changes to occur, but don't lose heart.

THE CHANGES WILL OCCUR!

Please know that the changes are now occurring even if they are not currently visible to you.

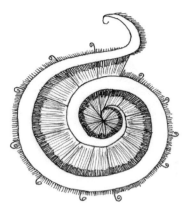

Let's apply this to an actual situation in your life:

- Take a moment now and explore a few ways that you can immediately effect change by using your imagination.

- Develop a vision of yourself acting in the way that you want to act in your next encounter with your boss or a family member.

- Next, use your physical senses as a starting point toward building a stronger imagination.

- Envision what you are wearing. See yourself sitting at your desk or at a table.

- What would you like to have happen in this encounter? Be specific and focused.

- What would bring you joy, happiness, or peace?

Now reinforce your imaginative thoughts by taking physical action:

- Write down the words you are using in this encounter with your boss or family member while you are calm, cool, collected, and present.

- Now develop a vision of how you are going to feel in your next interaction with this other person. *Focus.* Feel what it's like to have your emotions in a place that *you* have chosen.

- Trust that what you are imagining from your heart is being created as you are imagining it. Keep your thoughts, heart, and mind on what it is that you want to manifest in your life.

- Make time to go inside and experience what it is you are truly feeling, for from every interaction, you have an opportunity for growth.

Breathe.

Relax.

Give yourself permission to acknowledge stuck energy and then activate your imagination to get it unstuck.

START FROM WHERE YOU ARE and apply the tool of imagination to your inner feelings and transmute them into something positive by changing your attitude and viewing additional possibilities.

Now, *release negative feelings* and experience a lightness of thought and body. Let go and feel the new possibilities.

Go back into the above encounter and use your sight, hearing, touch, taste, and smell to provide the richer details.

> *Understand that by this very exercise,*
> *you have already created change!*

Through the use of your imagination, you have shifted your energy. This shift will have an immediate and substantial effect in how you respond to your employer or family member.

> *Please know that when you start imagining*
> *something you are opening a space for it*
> *to exist in your material reality.*

Remember...

*It is through the use of your imagination
that you can open space or close space.*

*You can bring forth
and you can let go.*

*It is through using your imagination
that you make manifest or make dissolve.*

Think BIG

If your first thoughts are large and lush, but then you start to think, "Oh, no, this is too big, I need to ask for less," please *immediately* stop yourself!

Know that by allowing these limiting thoughts to intrude between you and your heart's desire, you are building or creating walls. Your doubt has an energy that acts as a filter to your receiving.

Instead, please continue to affirm the larger desire...

THE BIGGEST ONE YOU CAN IMAGINE!

*Allowing yourself to be childlike
and imagining in great abundance
will actually speed along the manifestation
of what you are imagining
because you are letting go of judgment.*

Take Steps

If it is more comfortable for you, you may first choose to imagine obtaining your heart's desire through a series of smaller steps, like the steps up to your dream home.

Listen to your *hunches* for what you need to do next, keeping your heart's desire open.

*Know that if your heart
is in harmony with your soul,
things happen immediately.*

They are not labor intensive. The actions you carry out follow the inner guidance you receive, the hunches you get.

As the universe is infinite,
so too is your imagination.

What you want is already there.

Allow it to occur in your life at this time. Say to yourself:

This or something greater, God.

Be grateful for where you are now.

Don't limit your self.

When you make it *smaller*, you *limit* your *SELF*,
and you put limits on God, because limitation
is not the Divine Mind's plan for you.

This limiting is your *three-dimensional mind*,
not your Divine Mind.

Imagination Energizes Intuition

Intuition is something that many people have been conditioned to ignore. Intuitive senses, hunches, and *gut feelings* too often take a back seat to pure logic.

The imagination is a flowing, intuitive organism.

Tapping into your instincts is key to developing a healthy imagination.

Whenever you have a hunch,
take a moment to jot it down.

- Write out your hunch in as much detail and description as you can.

- Use adjectives and adverbs to expand the picture.

- Be sure to include aromas, fragrances, sounds, colors, and movement.

When you have a chance to look back and examine the details of the situation, write a few sentences about your hunch. Write about how accurate, how strong, and how useful it would be if you acted on it— or how useful it would be if you did not act upon it.

Keep a record of all your strong hunches so that you can go back and study them at your leisure.

Meditation Supports Imagination

Meditation is also an excellent way to free your mind. When you reach a state of mental relaxation, your imagination is free to expand and flow.

Some metaphysical folks consider the physical world, or plane, to be very base. They would like us to think that the body and the experiences of the body aren't as important as the mind.

*Scientific studies show
that there is an intimate relationship
between the mind and the body.*

You imagine with BOTH the body and the mind. Physical activity can bring inspiration, and your five senses can bring you into a highly receptive mental state. Similarly, imagination can bring real, physical results. By following through on your dreams, you can create the world in which you want to be.

*It is your imagination which first
brings to consciousness the facets of your inner being.*

Imagination Is Powerful

When you have imagined what it is that you would like manifested in your life, please send your thoughts and pictures off with the following words:

Under Grace, in a perfect way,
I release you to be wonderfully created
and I open my arms wide to allow you
into my life with ease and joy.

By using these words, you are freeing all thought forms and allowing the Source to *create*. Please know that these words are vital.

By freeing the thought forms, you have made a space
to receive even more of what you desire.

In this imagination phase, we always want to be open to receiving more than we can imagine so that each time we imagine, we feel good and comfortable—we grow and expand!

Please be aware that through this imaginative process, you are linking your heart's desires with GRACE, with the highest levels of Creation.

It is through your personal will or thoughts that you are sending out your desires into the universe without filters. You are connecting with the Creative Force, which will send these back to you with ease under Grace.

Your imagination is in service to your
divine plan, your greater good.

You have learned how activating your imagination brings color to your life, and... it is through the use of your imagination and your willingness to be open that you may explore and recognize your inner feelings.

When you go inside, your imagination and your senses provide you with impressions of texture, sound, material, color, and movement. These impressions will help you to *expand* your senses, *expand* your understanding, and *expand* all the feelings that may be inside of you.

As your perception of the physical world is modified or broadened, limits upon your imagination are loosened.

Imagery and senses become more robust.
The world around you
becomes painted in vibrant colors and
becomes a place which invites exploration.

Your language begins to reflect the *possibilities* instead of the *limitations*.

- You begin to live in possibilities rather than restrictions.
- Your view of yourself and your world changes.
- There are openings.
- You begin to see yourself differently, in a larger way.

ACTIVATING YOUR IMAGINATION—is it that easy? I merely envision an opening of space for the imagined event to occur.

Is it really that easy?
Well, yes and no.

Yes, imagining the event or occurrence of something
you want to manifest in your life is the first step.

Then activating your imagination and putting *focus* on what you want to occur means that you remember to imagine and that you are willing to allow all of your senses to be involved.

Colors, textures, and different kinds of materials are real in your imagination. When you take a pencil drawing and use colors and shading, you bring it to life.

Take a moment now and imagine something that you long for, something that you have been dreaming about.

- Using your imagination, give texture to this image as well as depth and color.
- Now put yourself in the picture.
- Imagine how you would act.
- See yourself doing what you desire.
- Feel it to be real.

Activating your imagination can lead to a newly-enhanced passion for life.

You were brought forth through divine energy
to exist as a CREATIVE BEING.

You are a beautiful LIGHT BEING
full of possibilities, love and wonder.

An Active Imagination Provides a Myriad of Potential Paths for Your Life.

One of the greatest uses of your time is time spent using the gift of imagination. Imagination expands your possibilities and your mind beyond the logical and scientific into a realm where your dreams can come true.

Know that the body and the mind
should be equal and balanced
for mental, physical, and spiritual health.

Please become a more engaged participant in your life through encouraging your imagination to be fertile, active, and boundless.

Realize that the use of your imagination
—the way that you think and perceive—
creates the reality that you experience.

Use your imagination to follow through on your dreams to create the kind of life activities which are loving, joyful, interesting, and satisfying to you.

The exercises, affirmations, guided imageries, and meditations found at the end of this chapter were designed to assist you to activate your imagination.

Tools to activate your imagination include thought, visualization, journaling, meditating, and frequently speaking aloud the affirmations at the end of this chapter.

Joy is waiting for you!

Activating Your Imagination:
ACTIVITIES

ACTIVATING YOUR IMAGINATION can be both fun and exciting. Allow your mind and emotions to roam free. See open doors instead of blank walls. Employing all your senses, visualize in rich colors, varying textures, and a myriad of scents.

For a few of you, unleashing your imagination may at first be a little scary as perhaps you haven't allowed yourself to use your imagination in some time.

To start, imagine that you have just bitten into a very sour pickle. What happened in your mouth?

Your thoughts and imagination brought about a *physical response*. While the pickle imagery was simple, science has proven that imagination can alter your very cell structure. I ask that as you work through these exercises and start re-activating your imagination, you permit yourself to use your imagination to put thoughts and ideas together that may not as yet make sense.

Give your imagination free reign.

1. Using your imagination, think of a warm, rich, loving, place full of colors, tones, vibrations, smells, feelings, and textures. Please write a paragraph on what you are now feeling in your heart. Please write a paragraph on what you are feeling in your belly. Are they the same? What are the differences, if any?

2. Using your imagination, think of an inner quality that you have admired in someone. Imagine yourself with that quality. Please write a paragraph on how having that quality would affect your life. Write it in the present tense: I *have this wonderful inner quality of...* Please write a paragraph on how having that quality would affect the lives of those you care for.

_____

_____

_____

_____

_____

_____

_____

_____

_____

_____

_____

_____

_____

_____

_____

_____

_____

_____

_____

_____

_____

_____

_____

3. Using your imagination, think about spring. Act as if it is now next spring. Imagine nature in bloom and a time of rebirth. Using your imagination, write down where and what you will be doing next spring. Remember to put action in your picture.

4. Using your physical senses assists you in awakening the consciousness of your imagination. The next time you have a chance, pick up a piece of fruit. Use your senses. Look at the fruit. Touch the skin of the fruit. Is it soft? Is it hard? Is it smooth or is it rough? Now smell it. Is it sweet or bitter? Does it smell tangy? Now open the fruit. What do you see? Does it smell different? Does it feel different? What is the sound when it was opened? Did it sound crisp? Did it squelch? Did it sound juicy? Now taste it with your eyes closed. Now taste it with your eyes opened. Is there a difference? If so, what?

_____

_____

_____

_____

_____

_____

_____

_____

_____

_____

_____

_____

_____

_____

_____

_____

5. There exists a connection between words and thought.
    Write your first thoughts to the following words:

    JOY

    _____

    GREATNESS

    _____

    RED VELVET

    _____

    LUSHNESS

    _____

    MORNING TIDE

    _____

    ABUNDANCE

    _____

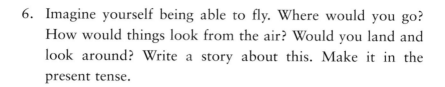

6. Imagine yourself being able to fly. Where would you go? How would things look from the air? Would you land and look around? Write a story about this. Make it in the present tense.

7. Imagine yourself having a day that you consider to be perfect. How does your day go? Who do you spend time with? Where are you? Remember the sky is endless and so is your imagination. Embellish it. Make it BIG. Make it in the NOW.

8. Imagine yourself on a wonderful vacation. Is it warm or cold? Are you alone? Is it peaceful or noisy? Do you find that you are limiting yourself to only those things which are practical or possible?

_____

_____

_____

_____

_____

_____

_____

_____

_____

_____

_____

_____

_____

_____

_____

_____

_____

_____

_____

_____

_____

_____

_____

Final Thoughts

- Follow the principles, being truthful with yourself at all times.

- Allow your imagination to develop.

- Give yourself the time you need.

- Be grateful and give praise for what is in your life now and what is being drawn to you as you learn the steps.

- Have fun!

- Allow yourself to be childlike.

- Explore.

- Be silly.

- Experience more richness in your life.

Activating Your Imagination:
AFFIRMATIONS

The Importance of Saying It Out Loud

THE THROAT CHAKRA is the fifth of the seven chakras of the body. It is the center of creativity to bring the Source forward in the three-dimensional world.

The throat chakra is where the creation of sound begins, and the sound continues from the throat chakra through our alphabet. These sounds vibrate and open the Source. These words and sounds form patterns, opening the doors for dreams, wishes and desires to manifest.

Each language, having its own vibrational patterns, allows the Source to manifest in its own way. The way we were created as beings of God was through sound. That sound became words, and those words become praise to God.

We are truly praise to God.

Affirmations

*I allow my imagination to wander
in bright fields of golden light nourishing
me with a sense of accomplishment and joy.*

Vibrant colors now color my black and white life.

*I am an abundant stream of new ideas
as all that I see is magical and reflects goodness.*

*Love Light and Truth now flow through me,
opening the channels of my creativity.*

*As I allow my imagination to soar,
my day-to-day life is transformed in a magical way.*

*The many-faceted jewels of my imagination
now shine rightly in the deep recesses of my mind.*

I expect and look with wonder at the miracles in my day.

*The greatest love of my heart streams forth
opening all good possibilities for my life.*

*The wonder of my imagination
brings forth great delights.*

*I am open and receptive to all good images
that I see, feel and sense.*

*My imagination invents lovely creations
full of light and delight.*

How to Make our Affirmations More Effective

- Affirmations are best stated over and over again, in the *present tense*, with conviction, authority and belief.

- They can even be sung to clear the old programming.

- The new statements will change your thinking and create a new positive reality. In days past all prayers were sung to give more energy and openness to receive goodness.

- Try making a song out of your affirmation. Speaking affirmations out loud reprograms our subconscious mind.

- Saying or singing affirmations begins to dissolve or reprogram negative thought patterns. Affirmations create new *open* patterns of receptivity. Affirmations help develop the intuition.

- Affirmations should be opened and closed by speaking out loud the following words:

Under Grace and in a perfect way...

By divine right...

My divinely chosen desire is given to me now under Grace and in a perfect way. So be it. So it is. Amen.

These words take worry away because they reinforce that the details are being taken care of by God, the Source.

- Saying, *God's will not my will,* opens up possibilities in ways we know not of.

- It brings us from the *limited* to the *limitless.*

  Saying *under Grace* opens love and removes karma or cause and effect.

- When we say, under Grace, we are asking to be lifted up and to be seen as God sees us, with unconditional love. This love can then work to dissolve *cause and effect* and bring great love to you.

Create Your Own Affirmations

Please feel free to create your own affirmations. Just remember that affirmations are *creating energy patterns* which are being sent forth to be fulfilled.

Your affirmations must be positive. Use the "I am" format, and stay in the present tense. By this, I mean what is happening at this moment.

The subconscious mind works as if everything is happening in the NOW.

Start your affirmation with *now* words. For example: "I am appreciated at my job today." "I am talented." "I am financially stable." "I am able to provide for my family now."

Make sure your words don't imply that the event will take place in the future. Instead of saying, "I will be rich," say, "I am rich NOW."

Using the present tense allows your inner resources to move the entire universe to manifest what you want in your life now.

When you say, "I am going to be rich soon," you are putting intentions out there that you are not ready for riches *NOW*. Your words are keeping your riches at bay.

When you use words which are negative such as, "I am never going to get a job," you are commanding that to be real. Think about the words you use daily...

While the repetition of affirmations does not, in and of itself, expand your awareness, what it does is clear the negative filters that keep you from obtaining your heart's desire. The repetitions magnetize you to activate your divine pattern—what is in harmony with your heart's desires.

If you catch yourself using negative words, immediately cancel by saying, "Cancel, cancel, cancel" or "Erase, erase, erase," thereby commanding the Universe to dissolve those forms and patterns of the ill-spoken words.

Please remember to put affirmations in the *I AM* format, at least at first.

I AM is the name of God.

When you understand that *I AM* is a literal command to the Universe, whatever you connect to the *I AM* will be made so in the three-dimensional world.

Your Own Affirmations:
JOURNAL

Your Own Affirmations:
JOURNAL

Activating Your Imagination:
MEDITATIONS

PLEASE GET COMFORTABLE. Breathing down to your belly, take your attention down inside and allow the soft part of your abdomen to go in and out with each long, slow breath. Follow your breath. Allow each breath to take you deeper inside. Become aware of what you are feeling in the moment.

Please become aware of your thoughts, feeling, ideas, and structures, which are normally silent during your day-to-day activities.

Observe without evaluation or judgment.

Be present and allow your imagination to be active.

Employing your senses of sight, touch, smell, taste, and hearing, consider the suggestions below as possible beginnings for you to place your focus. When you are finished with your meditation, please write down in your journal pages what it is that you perceive.

1. **SPACE MEDITATION**

    Using your imagination, go to a place. The place may be real or imagined. Go into the place and look around. What is the smell and texture? Are you standing or sitting? Is the air stirring? Where are you? Who are you? What are you seeing in the environment. How are you dressed? How do you feel? Is this exercise easy or hard?

2. **MUSIC MEDITATION**

    Listen to music with your eyes closed or focused on a sight that is pleasing to you. Now look inward: What emotions are you feeling? What images come into your mind? Can you expand your feelings? Where do they take you?

3. **LOVE MEDITATION**

    Imagine the color of cotton candy. Imagine the softness of the finest velvet. As you breathe, I would like you to see these as the greatest love you have experienced. Now breathe that love into you with every breath, so you inhale and exhale love. Breathe love into every part of your body starting with the little toes of your feet and working upwards until you reach the top of your head. Note your feelings as you breathe. Can you breathe love into the room where you are seated? Keep expanding your imagination until you breathe love into your community, state, country, and the whole world. How do you feel now?

*IMAGINATION
IS THE FIRST TOOL
THAT ONE NEEDS
TO MANIFEST OR CREATE
WHAT WILL BE.*

Activating Your Imagination:
GUIDED IMAGERY

PLEASE TAKE A MOMENT, get comfortable, take a few deep breaths, and allow your mind to expand and to go into places that it may never have gone before.

It takes work to expand your consciousness so that you may begin to lengthen those times of insight and bliss, so that you can then begin to believe the messages that reside there for you—and then to always remember and trust...

1. Imagine you are on the beach, in a field, or in the mountains. It has been a rainy day and the sun is just coming out but about to set. The rays of light are piercing through the atmosphere and energizing the small mist that is left from the rain, opening the great spectrum of light. Allow yourself to see and feel all the colors displayed by nature, reminding you of the infinite colors and shades of the world.

2. Imagine that you are in a spring meadow. The wind is blowing through the trees and you hear the sound of the breeze. The blades of grass are rubbing together, gently moving in harmony. The trees add to this symphony through the soft motion of the leaves and branches. Imagine all these sounds gently nourishing the places in your body. Imagine these sounds coming into your body, reminding you of the gentle loving sounds of nature.

3. Imagine you are in a very dense forest with ancient trees, perhaps the ancient redwoods. It is dark and you need to find your way through. See yourself asking for guidance. Feel the gentle movement of the ancient trees as they bend ever so slightly, getting closer to you to let you know which way to go. Feel the information gently brush on the skin of your face and feel your body calm as you allow the guidance of the ancient ones to show you the way.

Activating Your Imagination:
JOURNAL

Activating Your Imagination:
JOURNAL

DEVELOPING THE SKILL OF DISCERNMENT

Seeing Truth When Exploring Your Life Possibilities

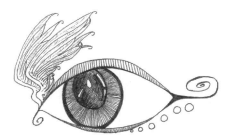

The knowledge you seek is already inside you.
Just remove what is hiding your knowing.

Discernment gives you the knowledge
of what will bring you to your highest good.

Discernment

TO DISCERN IS TO PERCEIVE or recognize one thing from another.

To discern is to make clear and recognize differences.

To discern is to develop your insight, your knowledge, your intuition and your recognition of the differences and shades of differences in the choices that are presented to you daily.

To discern is to separate Truth from untruth.

To discern is to begin to know differently, using what is inside of you to activate your spirit in a search for core purpose.

To discern is to begin to see what is clear and to let go of what is muddy or tainted or contrived or false.

When you actively use your skill of discernment, you make choices, you make decisions that are right and true for you. You make decisions from your heart—conscious and fully present. You make decisions that are a result of clear thought.

You then place your attention on what you now discern will bring you to your highest good.

Discernment is looking at gradations of differences in choices and possibilities present in your daily life.

Discernment is not intuition. Intuition is an inkling, a feeling that you may experience upon meeting someone for the first time or entering into a new environment.

Discernment is more than intuition.

Discernment is active.

Discernment utilizes and encompasses your intuition, your past knowledge, your intellect, your past experiences, and your education.

It asks you for a deeper understanding or a deeper sight that can only be gained from going within.

Discernment is using all that you have. It is bringing forward the parts of your being which "know" on levels you are not yet using in every day life.

*Discernment is a powerful tool to assist you
in achieving what you are seeking.*

What You Can Expect

Developing the skill of discernment will teach you how to know which of the many choices and possibilities available to you resonate as harmonious and *true for you.*

When you practice the skill of discernment you begin to open, to discover new parts of your *self.* This discovery, this unveiling, will lead you to a new understanding of *self,* including what you value when you are being true to your self.

When you have developed the skill of discernment,
you are present with yourself.

You see what is really there.

You will find that the more your inner self is revealed, the more your sense of connection, of wonderment, of peace and of joy will grow.

Practice of Discernment

AS IMPORTANT AS THE REVELATION of your true self is, it is in practicing the art of discernment that will bring you from a world of grinding work with limited possibilities to a world wide open and full of possibilities.

You will begin to experience your wishes
coming into existence in a material way.

Now, this is very important because we live in a material world, we are here to manifest spirit in matter.

As you develop your skill of discernment, your intuition, your inner guidance system, you will be putting into play some very powerful principles.

These principles are principles of Truth.

You will begin to give energy to your inner desires.

Inner Truth

> *What is meant by giving your inner Truth energy?*

This means that you make valid what you discern to be truthful for you, you validate your inner knowing instead of what others may believe or decide should be your Truth.

> *Stop a moment here.*
> *Think about the last time someone*
> *asked you for your inner Truth.*

Using the skill of discernment is allowing yourself to begin to observe your inner *self*, to know yourself.

Can you recall the last time you went inside yourself and asked yourself for the whole unadulterated Truth?

> *When you practice discernment,*
> *you will pay attention to and consider the places*
> *within yourself that show you the way*
> *and provide you with the Truth of who you are*
> *and where you are going.*

New Perspective

When you take action based on discerned revelations, you gain a new perspective of value. You act from a place of validity in your life, making time in your daily activities to work on your goals. You begin to depend on your inner Truth as a basis for who you are and what you are about.

Your discernment will tell you what you need to do to bring you to your *Highest Good*. You start to build a sense of self-esteem because you are finally considering your *SELF*.

Know that as your path is shown, more of who you are is also revealed.

You begin to understand what is necessary.

There may be much work involved, but this is work that is guided through your discernment.

It is a joyous activity. It is energizing.

You will not find this work to be drudgery because you will know that this is work you will be performing with an openness. It is motivating and interesting. You are listening, which keeps you alert to your divine possibilities.

You Benefit Through Discernment

You all know of the many books being sold that tell you how to be a millionaire or how to marry the person of your dreams or how to be at the top of your field.

You may find some of the tips or strategies in some of these books very useful. However, in order to gain the full benefit of these books—to increase the joy in your life—it is vital that you develop the skill of discernment, for it is in discernment that your inner Truth tells you what approach will work for you, what road to take.

You will now know that you have within you
the capability to know answers,
to know choices, to know possibilities.

Look At What You Gain

You see yourself as the magnificent being that you truly are
the multi-faceted, infinitely energized being of God.

Because you are now working toward the goals of your heart, you are working with focus, with energy, with a knowing that changes the whole way you feel and move.

You are not just going through the motions of life. Life is not what is happening to you or all around you.

You are the active participant as well as the active observer.

You are now open to receive God's light.

With intuition and discernment, the events of life are viewed as interesting puzzles. You know the good that is in your future. You know that any seemingly negative event is actually for your good. It is an opportunity to succeed.

You need lessons to monitor your growth so that you can see the progress you are making in achieving your hearts' desires. You are then able to have more loving acceptance of yourself.

When you use your skill of discernment, you will notice that you are going below the surface. You will find that decisions are multi-layered. As you start this process, you begin to change your world view because as you focus, shifts occur.

You see further the path of where each decision would take you. You see more clearly, and through your imagination you find that you will ask yourself more meaningful questions.

Your mind and heart are working together
for a wondrous gift—YOU.

You are Truly the Expert

You are changing your world view. You are beginning to consider yourself the first authority or expert on your life.

This shift in itself is revolutionary.

You stop seeking answers or expertise from the outside and shift to your inside. You may read books, attend lectures to learn tools, but they don't know who you are.

Inside, you know who you are!
The knowledge of who you are is inside.

You will feel a sense of anticipation of things, that good things are happening. You are taking the Truth and using the Truth in your life rather than using outside constructs that are supposed to work but that in essence won't work and are superficial.

Activate Your Discernment

INTUITION IS AN INFLOW of inspiration, ideas, and imagination. When you are discerning, you are actively looking for the path or the choice. Intuition is the inkling you may call upon when you use discernment, but discernment is the practical tool.

Using your imagination and your intuition, consider what you wish to create in your life. Remember to ask yourself...

Are my decisions harmonious with what I really am inside?

This is important!
Ask **AGAIN.**

Are my decisions harmonious with what I really am inside?
What decisions do I really need to make?

To Thine Own Self Be True

Being true to yourself is powerful and affirming.

There may be several *right* decisions.

When you use discernment,
you will know that your choice is right, or truthful,
because it will resonate with your heart.

Opening the doors to your heart is how God works best through you.

You have the ability to know Truth by going into your heart.

A right decision clears a path or opens a vista so that
you are able to see a place beyond where you are now.

You begin to have insight into those actions which will lead you to that place that you have visualized, a place that is your highest good.

PLEASE REMEMBER

Truth feels good.

Truth feels happy.

Truth is peaceful.

Truth is refreshing.

Developing the skill of discernment
allows you to make decisions from a truthful place.

Using the Skill of Discernment in Practical Matters

- What position or job should I have in the workforce?

- Where will I be able to make a difference?

- What sort of skills am I interested in?

- Where will I be valued and recognized and able to bring a sense of accomplishment and growth?

- Where should I live?

- Who am I meant to be with?

- How do I find a partner?

- What qualities in a partner will reflect the qualities inside of me?

- What will bring me to be a better person?

- What will actively stimulate me to be all I can be?

- What route do I need to take?

- How do I talk to my boss?

- How do I have a better relationship with my partner?

- How do I speak so that others hear me—my kids, my boss, my partner, my parents, my friends, those with whom I wish to share?

- How do I take better care of my health?

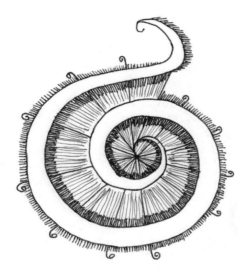

In using this new skill of discernment, think of it as a muscle in your body. At first you have to work to build it, using it as the need arises.

You condition yourself and continue building the skill, using it and refining it, bringing it to a higher level so that you do not have to consciously say, "Now I will use the skill of discernment."

You automatically call on your heart to say, "Is this good for me?"

Your heart automatically opens to you,
giving you more insight and information
regarding the highest and best path to take.

Let's Practice

To begin: When you bring a possibility into your heart, ask yourself the following questions…

- What do I feel?

- Am I feeling calm?

- Am I feeling peaceful?

- Do I have a feeling of joy? of rightness?

Steps in Using the Skill of Discernment

Maybe you are not at ease or filled with joy or calmness. Because you are being cared for by God, the Source, and the angels, they are informing you that the path you are on is *not* for your highest good. They want you to know there are other paths that are better for you.

Come back into your heart and ask, "From where or from whom is this feeling coming?

> *When your thoughts or choices leave you feeling*
> *anxious or frustrated, then it is time to stop and ask,*
> *"Are these my feelings or do they belong to someone else?"*

By this I mean, are these the feelings of another that you have taken on? Go into your heart—Is this really your feeling? Is it there by fear, by fear of the unknown?

> *Listen to your feelings.*

They are important tools in mastering the art of discernment.

It is mastering the art of discernment which shows you the pathway to well-being.

Please allow whatever comes from you to be valid.

This is vital to growth. Explore, contribute, participate, and know that your inner self is safe. Allow what is within you to come forward and be part of the experience without judgment.

Let your innocence,
your freedom from the judgment of others,
be present, heard, and activated.

Innocence places you into a state of Grace where miracles happen. When you come back to innocence, you come back to the Source and see Truth. Innocence is a state of bliss.

Possibilities and Discernment

Please consider that you are faced with several possibilities, some of which may lead to the same or similar outcome, but other possibilities may lead to potentially very different outcomes.

What do you call upon to assist you in making a decision about which possibility to pursue?

Do you listen and call upon...

> your feelings, instincts,
> intuitions, past experiences
> and certain gut level reactions?

Developing the skill of discernment enables you to distinguish those *intuitions* and *insights* which when acted upon by you are...

> always true
> mostly true
> sometimes true
> mostly not true
> or never true for you.

Look Deeper

One key skill in learning to discern what is right for you and what will bring you to your highest good is learning where you may have developed biases and what these biases are based on.

Take a moment now to jot down some important things that you hold as fact in your life.

_____

_____

_____

_____

_____

_____

_____

_____

Explore beliefs that are central to you that you treat as fact.

It is key to ask yourself, "Is each of the beliefs I hold as Truth a fact or a societal norm? "

Ask if each of these beliefs is true for me, the inner me, or did I ascribe to these to fit in and be accepted?

Did I just grow up and accept what others believed?

Looking deeper is vital!

Intuition

Einstein said, *"Intuition is greater than REASON."* The person who lives life through intuition lives life in a state of Grace. Intuition allows one to defy the three-dimensional laws and make things happen that are seemingly impossible. Using intuition is key in creating a sense of joy.

Intuition can be a thought or feeling that comes to you out of the blue. It can also be part of your inner guidance that you call upon when making decisions. Have you ever wanted to find out some information and the thought occurs to you out of the blue where to go and what to act upon?

This is your intuition.

Do you ever just have a sense about something that really can't be explained?

This is your intuition.

Do you ever have a gut feeling about something?

This is your intuition.

It's important to allow intuition to have a place in your life. It needs to be taken by you with a sense of validation. Indeed, perhaps you need to give permission to yourself to be conscious of what your intuition is conveying to you.

Please take a moment now to give yourself permission to be with your intuition. How does it feel to allow intuition into your life?

_____

_____

_____

_____

Go Overboard with Intuition

Another key to developing discernment is allowing your intuition to have free reign. So often intuition is ignored for something more *reasonable.* We tend to *worship logic* and *demean intuition.* However, life does not operate logically.

As we become more familiar with how intuition feels inside, we begin to use it more.

Those feelings that you have when you first meet someone need to be observed with discernment.

Could these feelings be intuition?

Discernment Is Vital to Manifestation

It is vital to developing your skill of discernment to go inside yourself.

It is inside each of us that the Truth resides.

This statement is very important to your being able to manifest.

It is from inside that you hold the knowledge of who you are and what you need and the direction you need to go. It is a Truth that manifests itself via instincts, intuition, and knowledge gained through our experiences since birth.

Intuition is defined as the direct perception of Truth.

Through intuition we are in touch with our Source.

It is an inner teaching by our Source.

Beings of Light

We, as beings of Light, function through our consciousness of our own Truth.

We are built on Truth.

The Truth is that we are meant to have self-love—self-esteem—for this is God's plan for us.

We are meant to be MAGNIFICENT HUMAN BEINGS at one with nature and each other—full of love, life and Truth regardless of our religious beliefs, our race, our gender, our socio-economic status.

Your being is apart from these.

See the Truth of your being, go forward, developing faith and courage. As you go forth in Truth, the universe will open up avenues for you that previously had appeared impossible.

Intuition, indeed, is far greater than knowledge.

Discover New Possibilities

Using your imagination facilitates the discovery of new possibilities. Using your skills of discernment you may choose from possibilities which will serve your highest good, and discover which Truths are indeed true for you.

Which new possibilities resonate with
well-being, joy, and happiness?

Developing the skill of discernment and then using discernment when making choices presents you with opportunities to explore what may have been until now uncharted territories.

Using discernment to search out nuances and differences may yield precious gold within the self that facilitates knowledge of who you are, what you are about, and how to operate in your highest good.

Actively using your imagination
and your skill of discernment is key
to getting your heart's desires to manifest.

To bring to life your dreams, wishes, and desires requires you to be able to determine the differences between what you actually have and what you will need to do to obtain what you want.

Discernment is that skill, which, when practiced,
facilitates your ability to see the gradation of differences
in the possibilities that are available to you each day.

You Are Unique

What makes you uniquely you?

Once you have learned what goes into your decision-making, examine how you perceive life's choices and how you can discern which choices are true for you.

Developing discernment leads to developing that faith and trust that may have been lying dormant.

Discernment may be an awakening of what is within and what helps you to focus your perception of the way in which your reality functions.

> *Getting to know your Self and what lies within*
> *starts the process of discernment.*

Discernment demands that you switch from an outside focus of attention to an inside focus. Become reacquainted with your *Self,* with your various sensations and the various intuitions that flow naturally from *Self.*

> *You will find an abundance of feelings*
> *and previously hidden understandings.*

> *Discernment is personal.*

Discernment in Wellness

You have already learned that your imagination is a powerful tool in your state of wellness. Now you will learn that following your insights and practicing the skill of discernment are also powerful tools in your state of wellness.

You begin to delineate what is *you* from what is *not you*.

This may seem a simple statement, but let's examine it more closely.

- How do you know who you are?
- How have you learned who you are?
- What is it like to go inside?
- By going inside you, what is it that you are aware of?

Taking on energy from others often happens
when you are in sympathy with them.

Is what you're feeling really yours? Most of the time you don't realize that you may be taking on another's energy.

This happens in a very subtle manner.

This energy is foreign, and your system and your being, while trying to incorporate it, are thrown out of balance. Taking on another's energy causes stress to your system that often goes unnoticed until a crisis of some sort occurs.

With this crisis comes the collapse of the system
because the system was not based on Truth.

The skill of discernment then needs to be employed to find the Truth in your energy system and to *let all else be dissolved.*

These other energies, as they are dissolved, allow more room for your *Divine Pattern* to draw energy from the Source, to fuel your enthusiasm for going forward, and breaking through barriers to manifesting what it is you desire.

A vibrant life, which can be achieved through combining *your* active imagination with a keen *sense of discernment...*

...creates timing
...opens the possibilities
...and presents previously unknown opportunities.

Allow yourself to experience the opportunities.

Go Into Your Heart

As you are going into your heart and learning what is true for you and what this feels like, you begin to understand yourself from a DIVINE place.

> *A more divine perspective with love and joy and happiness starts to manifest as you practice learning to know yourself.*

As you free yourself from what society has dictated for you, you connect with your *core essence*. You learn what it is that will lead you to joy and happiness. You also learn what is creating *disharmony* and *dis-ease* within you

Once you have learned the skill of discernment, there is no way that you can go down the wrong path, because your inner guidance system shows you step-by-step where you need to go from moment-to-moment.

It is no longer so fearful to start down a new path. Yes, it still takes courage, but the fear is tempered with the knowledge gained through discernment. Further, each success breeds another success and gives you added energy in seeking what is for your higher good.

You then may start to heal yourself and
become what you dream of becoming.

It is in each one of us to be wise,
to know what it is that we are here to accomplish.

Practicing the skill of discernment and acting with intuition
and insights can lead to a fuller, richer, happier life.

Developing the skill of discernment
will help you to realize your highest good.

Beyond Your Five Senses

Using discernment is more than using your five senses.

When making choices with your skill of discernment—in addition to using your senses—you use your heart, your head, and your gut.

In developing your skill of discernment, you develop your intuition. You begin to develop trust and faith. It is intuition which is your inside pipeline to the Source, to God.

You then begin to live *outside the three-dimensional world*—in the higher dimensions—where *Grace* is active in your life.

You will then achieve the impossible on a regular basis, bringing magic and wonderment back to your every day activities.

- People will be drawn to you.
- You will be open to what is for your highest good.

As the impossible becomes not just the possible but rather the regular daily occurrence, you come to expect and receive the impossible and are always delighted with how much more wonderful is each occurrence.

*Please become a positive participant in your life
through making wise choices.*

Acknowledge that you already have the ability to discern those Truths which are right for you. It is up to you to utilize and exercise the skills and tools of discernment, so that you develop a keen perception when making life's decisions.

*Realize and experience daily the power and security that comes
from exercising discernment when faced with life's choices.*

Tools to assist you in developing the skill of discernment include:

- thought
- journaling
- meditating
- affirmations
- practice

Joy is waiting for you.

Developing the Skill
of Discernment:
<u>ACTIVITIES</u>

TO DEVELOP THE SKILL of discernment is to develop your ability to *look inside* and gain insight of what is true for you.

It is to be able to look for *what is yourself* and *what is not yourself.*

What you accept as true for you may not be true for others.

It is letting go of that which is not for your higher good.

Developing the skill of discernment means
being able to go inside and recognize clearly
the differences between possibilities.

How Do You Know What You Know

To build your skills of discernment you should explore *how you know what you know* and what you utilize when you are making decisions.

You know that part of your knowledge derives from what you were taught from external sources such as school, your family, your religious beliefs, your peers, and the media.

For this exercise, please explore that part of your knowing which you believe comes free of external bias.

> *Explore that part of your knowing*
> *—your instincts and insights—*
> *which are the voice of your inner Truth.*

1. What did it feel like when you had a "gut" level reaction or feeling to a person or an idea?

2.   At this point in your life, what do you know about yourself:

MENTALLY

_____

_____

_____

_____

_____

_____

_____

EMOTIONALLY

_____

_____

_____

_____

_____

_____

_____

_____

SPIRITUALLY

_____

_____

_____

_____

_____

_____

_____

3. Look at your responses above. Do you see what *Inner Sources* you call upon when making decisions?

_____

_____

_____

_____

_____

_____

_____

_____

_____

_____

_____

_____

_____

_____

_____

_____

_____

_____

_____

_____

_____

_____

_____

4. Please complete the following sentence: *It will benefit me to call upon my skill of discernment when choosing ...*

5. Getting to know your skill of discernment, what sorts of things do you know that are mostly true? Sometimes true? Always true? Usually not true? Always not true?

6. Take time now to note what are the different sensations, intuitions, inklings, and hunches that go with the above gradations of Truth.

_____

_____

_____

_____

_____

_____

_____

_____

_____

_____

_____

_____

_____

_____

_____

_____

_____

_____

_____

_____

_____

_____

Developing the Skill
of Discernment:
AFFIRMATIONS

*I have the ability within myself to discern, to know the
difference between what is true for me and what is not.*

All the things that I seek in my heart are now seeking me.

*I now see clearly what is before me in my divine good,
for my divine good.*

*I am sensitive and responsive to all good in my life
and I let go of all that does not belong to me.*

*I see clearly what is before me
and I am completely equipped to follow through.*

*I am completely prepared and totally equipped
to do what is mine to do today.*

*I am completely aware of what is good for me and I let
go of anything that is not of divine love.*

*I am seeing all that is.
I am seeing all the channels that are my **good**
open to me now and I am able right now
to know which path to follow.*

What is true of God is true of me. I know it to be so.

*I allow myself to feel the wonderful textures of my soul,
and I become aware of Truth.*

I follow my golden path of enlightenment.

Your Own Affirmations:
JOURNAL

Your Own Affirmations:
JOURNAL

Developing the Skill
of Discernment:
MEDITATIONS

PLEASE GET COMFORTABLE. Breathing down to your belly, take your attention down inside and allow the soft part of your abdomen to go in and out with each long, slow breath.

Follow your breath.

Allow each breath to take you deeper inside. Allow your mind to expand. Become aware of what you are feeling in this moment.

Become aware of your thoughts, feeling, ideas, and structures which are normally silent during your day-to-day activities.

Observe without evaluation or judgment.

Be present and observe what is really true for you.

Employing your senses of sight, touch, smell, taste, and hearing, below are some suggestions of possible beginnings for you to place your focus. When you are finished with your meditation, please jot down what it is that you perceive.

1. *Go inside and search your mind, heart, and spirit for that place which has been kept so secret that it may even be hidden from you.* What is your treasure? Using your intuition, your heart, and imagination, sift through possibilities to see how to arrive at your treasure.

2. Use this meditation as a key to higher development of mind, body, and spirit. Assist yourself to develop clear sight. Develop an ability to see beyond the surface—to perceive what is truly there. Keep your eyes open to new ideas and experiences. Bathe the possibilities in light. *LOOK AND SEE WHAT EMERGES.* Use the light from heaven as a meditation. See what Truth shines through.

_____

_____

_____

_____

_____

_____

_____

_____

_____

_____

_____

_____

_____

_____

_____

_____

_____

_____

_____

_____

3. Take time in this mediation to acknowledge every cell in your body for being the magnificent presence that allows you to have this physical experience on earth. Start with your feet and work up.

Pay attention to the messages that are being given and shown to you in each of your cells as they gather into *tissues, organs, organ systems,* and *your amazing DIVINE body.*

Developing the Skill
of Discernment:
GUIDED IMAGERY

PLEASE TAKE A MOMENT and get comfortable.

Breathe and allow your mind to expand and go into places that it *may never have gone before.*

It takes work to expand your consciousness, so that you may begin to lengthen those times of insight and bliss. You can then begin to believe the messages that reside there for you.

Remember...

Discern what it feels like inside when something is true for you all the time—versus only some of the time.

Start with something that you know is always true for you. Put this feeling inside. Breathe it in and breathe it out allowing your senses to expand around it. Bathe it in a beautiful light.

This is how you may go inside and know what is true for you.

1. You are in a large, confusing maze searching for a desired treasure. To be successful, you must utilize all your senses and trust your instincts. Please tease out what is not necessary and will not help you on your quest. You must be able to examine all your previous attempts with a fresh perspective, questioning what must be done differently in future attempts to obtain the treasure.

_____

_____

_____

_____

_____

_____

_____

_____

_____

_____

_____

_____

_____

_____

_____

_____

_____

_____

_____

_____

_____

_____

2. You are surrounded by nature—from a glorious golden sand or a rich, lush, green meadow. As you walk through nature, you see before you a series of paths. Which path do you take? What do you see on your journey? Are all paths to your good? What about the path that leads to a dead-end? How will you respond? Do you let it stop you? Do you retrace your steps?

_____

_____

_____

_____

_____

_____

_____

_____

_____

_____

_____

_____

_____

_____

_____

_____

_____

_____

_____

_____

_____

3. You are able to travel to the centers of your brain to conduct a meeting with each of the heads of each of the cortices of your brain. You flow through the neural pathways and you are able to notice the various debris and other kinds of patterns as you travel.

Through sending love from your heart, you are able to change what is on your neural pathway.

Please take notice of the color and texture as you travel and notice your thoughts and feelings along the way.

Developing the Skill of Discernment:
JOURNAL

Developing the Skill of Discernment:
JOURNAL

Love, Praise, Gratitude, and Appreciation

A kaleidoscope of possibilities shines through you, presenting a shimmering image and revealing the healthy rich fullness of your life.

LPGA

THE LESSON ON **"Living a Life in Love, Praise, Gratitude, and Appreciation"** is about living a life in which God's magnificent and shining blessings become apparent in our everyday lives.

It is the essence of your physical experience to amplify the spiritual experience, for you are a spiritual being having a physical experience.

> *Your heart's desire is God's desire for you*
> *and having an open heart is necessary*
> *to knowing what it is that God wants for you.*
>
> *Many people, unaware of this universal Truth,*
> *operate from the mind instead of the heart.*

The mind deals with the three-dimensional, logical, and rational states.

The heart operates in the non-physical state of love explaining the mysterious with great understanding.

- With heart, all things are possible.

- With heart, all can be known and appreciated.

- With heart, we can overcome what the mind says is impossible.

- With heart, we can see universally.

- With heart, we can love, we can praise, we can have gratitude. This is what the mind often refuses to acknowledge.

- With heart, we are multi-dimensional.

Learning and then living in *Love, Praise, Gratitude and Appreciation* allow you to operate from the heart. A heart that is opened deals in the non-physical, the realm beyond the three-dimensional to that which is poetic, loving, creative, and multi-dimensional.

To open your heart, to be able to receive,
is amplified when you are living in
Love, Praise, Gratitude and Appreciation.

Love

LOVE IS AS ESSENTIAL AS AIR AND WATER—love for a child, love for a partner, love for a pet, love for a friend.

PURE LOVE EXPANDS YOU and allows you a feeling of well-being and peace. Love has its own vibration and its own picture and pattern in the universe.

THOUGHTS AND FEELINGS OF LOVE CARRY OUTWARD.

LOVE ADDS TO YOU as a warm, wonderful frequency of life energy, opening and nourishing.

- Love nourishes every cell.

- Love dissolves negativity.

- Love gives us different vision.

- Love lifts up the soul to greater possibilities and understanding.

- Love, as an energy, has the power to transmute negative into positive.

All love produces vibrations
which bring you closer to your *Self*
and it is in *Yourself* that you reach God.

You become more interesting to yourself.

You need less outside stimulation
because you are happy with your *Self*.

With love, comes the allowance
to be free of your own filters,
and you can be completely free
in your own presence.

The feeling of belonging
and having a place in the world
and in the universe is fostered by love.

True love is love for self,
FOR SELF IS GOD
as we are created in God's image.

Praise

Praise is to give glory, to magnify, to give thanks.

Giving praise makes the positive grow so that you will begin to accept the positive in your life that has been created by you and your positive attitude.

You had a hand in creating this positive experience or positive opportunity.

Examine your life...

...Look for aspects of people, events, occasions, signs and intuitions, which you are able to honestly praise.

Giving praise and getting in the habit of giving praise, you will soon realize that there is more and more for you to give praise to.

Praise is the act of sending forth the goodness you see, sending forth the love and gratitude to others.

Praise is acknowledging the blessings
already present in your life.

Gratitude

Gratitude is...an attitude, a feeling, an idea, an activity and a way of living in this world.

Put your thumb and forefinger together and press hard. The small space between (even though it seems like there is no space) is *infinite* and still *less* than the blessings that are yours today.

> *Each of us has in our lives*
> *something for which we can be grateful.*

When you proclaim and acknowledge your gratitude for the blessings which have already manifested in your life, channels of abundance are created, opened, cleared and expanded.

When you speak words of gratitude you are offering thanks and prayers to God. You then begin to vibrate yourself to the tune of God, so God answers back to you—a wonderful tune, a song resonating through the universe, lustrous as a pearl, the pearl of wisdom.

Appreciation

Appreciation is the sensitive understanding, the knowing, and enjoying of the value or quality of what is in your life. Having appreciation for what is good in your life attracts more of the same.

APPRECIATE WHAT YOU HAVE. As you appreciate you open the doors for more of what you are appreciating to come in. Appreciation erases the negative.

This is an important concept. Think about this...

...If you truly and sincerely appreciate—with an open heart—the past negativity you may have generated is automatically transmuted.

Life isn't meant to be just a struggle to make ends meet.

*Take time NOW to look around and give value
and appreciation to what makes your life joyous.*

To *appreciate* is to feel a warmth of satisfaction and approval for what is in your life.

No matter what it is or where you start—
with appreciation you begin to raise the value of life
and consciously expand it.

In the spiritual realm you are saying to God, to the Source, that you are interested *in receiving more of the same*, and that you acknowledge what you do—always giving value to it.

Each of us has power, power to change the way we live in this world and how the world responds to our being.

LOVE

PRAISE

GRATITUDE

APPRECIATION

Living in LPGA

When *Love, Praise, Gratitude and Appreciation* are practiced together daily, a connection is formed with your higher Source on a level that is not possible any other way.

Channels are opened which allow God to work through you and for you—changing your very existence.

Every person needs strong, open channels to God.

A life lived in *Love, Praise, Gratitude and Appreciation* is a spiritual life—a practice for creating those channels for communicating with your Source, so that the Source will open its abundance in the way that is meaningful and loving for *You.*

Real World Benefits

When you live in *Love, Praise, Gratitude and Appreciation* the effect (the impact) you have on your reality and your environment is real and apparent.

> *You receive back the effect of your intentions.*

> *What you are placing out into the universe is returning magnified.*

Those around you begin to respond to your presence *differently*. You begin to feel differently about situations, so your reactions are different and will result in different outcomes.

Previous patterns of negativity and criticism slowly fade away.

You will begin to see new opportunities for growth and change from previously challenging people and situations—all because of the *Love, Praise, Gratitude and Appreciation* that you are sending forth.

Please know that as you treat others well, the way in which you conduct your life attracts goodness into your life.

You are telling the universe, "This is what I am." Therefore, what you are is what is vibrating and pulsating with energy out *into* the universe.

- Like is attracting like.

- Take stock of what is happening in your life right now.

- Treat with love, praise, gratitude and appreciation.

- Take a moment to jot down some thoughts now.

_____
_____
_____
_____
_____
_____
_____
_____
_____
_____
_____
_____
_____
_____
_____
_____
_____

Send Love Always

As you wake up each morning—as you are meeting someone for the first time—prior to entering a job interview—take a few minutes to focus on offering love to those along your path.

Sing out praise for what is for your HIGHEST GOOD.

Give gratitude for this coming day.

Practice in this way...

...Take a situation in which you are usually less comfortable and practice sending love. I like to visualize pink cotton candy. I first learned this many years ago from one of my wonderful spiritual teachers. Think love, send love mentally, see love, visualize love, breathe love, move love, and then be present and observe.

You will notice a shift.

When resolving conflicts, envision love. Fill the room with love. Others are unprepared for this type of positive energy which allows you to be fully *present* and agile, shifting moment to moment. Notice that sending love frees your energy and frees your life force.

Jot down your successes.

Living in a Higher Realm

Living in *Love, Praise, Gratitude and Appreciation* vibrates us into a higher realm of being which facilitates opening the mind to new possibilities. Viewing these new possibilities magnifies and multiplies the openings in wondrous ways.

Dedicate yourself to *Love, Praise, Gratitude and Appreciation*. Watch your words and give praise when you can—that, of course, includes praising yourself.

As you change your approach to living life, life changes its approach to giving to you.

You respond differently to others, and others respond differently to you. As you approach new challenges, previously unknown channels will open for you.

Your state of being is changed—
You start to live in Grace.

Grace

When you start living in *Love, Praise, Gratitude and Appreciation*, you begin to walk in Grace, for Grace is the reality of God.

Think of the state of Grace as a bridge.

Love, Praise, Gratitude and Appreciation are steps along the bridge.

Practicing *Love, Praise, Gratitude and Appreciation* brings you to stand in Grace. From there you are able to take yourself out of the realm of *cause and effect* and take yourself into a state of Grace where miracles will happen—where the illogical is allowed to occur, where your dreams may come true.

> *You can now attract your heart's desires.*

Even if it is not conscious to you, you have created a space through *Love, Praise, Gratitude and Appreciation* by which the *highest* and *best* solution may manifest in your life RIGHT NOW in the PRESENT MOMENT.

In Grace,
you are standing
in God's presence.

You invite more abundance.

You let go of scarcity.

You begin to fill
your life with GRACE.

Grace is that state
whereby things come
gently and magically,
sustaining a sense of ease,
fun and delight.

Filters

Many people believe that what you put out, you will have returned to you many-fold. Another way of saying this is:

What you send out returns to you.

You might find, however, that there is a wall that blocks your receiving what you send out. This wall may limit your connection to the Source—causing what I call an *energy filter*.

Know that you can have what is coming from your heart without causing harm to others. It is a misunderstanding that if you want something from the material world, it takes away from others. This belief is an *energy filter*.

With *Love, Praise, Gratitude and Appreciation*, you can dissolve the *filter of fear* and choose love.

This allows you to be aware of more possibilities for your life.

Practicing *Love, Praise, Gratitude and Appreciation* opens more room for the divine to intervene on your behalf—dissolving *energy filters* and bringing you much closer to God, the Source.

Take a moment to think about this now...

The universe is not finite.

Always ask, using the words, *Under Divine Right,* or *Under Grace,* so you are not taking from someone else.

When you receive your heart's desire,
you are actually opening space for someone else
to obtain their heart's desire.

If what you are asking for could cause harm to someone else, then it is not from your heart.

You are asking it to be so in a perfect way for all concerned.

You are allowing the universe, the Source, God, to move the mountains for you in its own way, without trying to direct it.

Your desire can be made manifest for you in the highest and best way.

This process of using *Love, Praise, Gratitude and Appreciation* develops your trust and expands your faith in life.

The interaction between the God in you and the larger God around you becomes an exciting and interesting dance.

This interaction is always intriguing and gives you a new appreciation of how infinitely faceted God is.

Whatever it is you ask for—as you ask for it in *Love, Praise, Gratitude and Appreciation*—you will receive infinitely so much more.

You have now expanded as a human being in your ability to love.

You have patience in your ability to see and understand in ways not thought of before—in ways that would have seemed impossible in earlier years. But now it is an everyday occurrence.

Life is exciting.

Growth is exciting.

Each day is a wonderful adventure.

Think Outside the Physical Box

God does not hold us in an image of our *imperfection* but rather in an image of *perfection*. Perfection in Greek means *already whole*. God sees us always as *already whole*.

As you practice seeing *Love, Praise, Gratitude and Appreciation*—as you give Grace to others—you vibrate at a *higher frequency*, which allows miracles and magic to occur.

When you learn and consistently practice thinking outside the physical realm, then you begin to have an understanding, a real love of the spiritual realm.

Your own spirituality will grow and go beyond something you do Sunday, or Saturday, or Friday night.

Your spirituality will be one with your every breath. You will experience a knowing, an understanding that you are more than just a *physical being*.

Your core and heart and mind and emotions
now flow from a different energy.

Your energy will be boosted so that
you move forth in a more fluid way.

God Makes A Way

God makes a way is one of my favorite affirmations.

PLEASE KNOW THAT THE WAY
HAS ALREADY BEEN MADE FOR YOU.

In your state of graciousness you are sending *Love, Praise, Gratitude and Appreciation* without a preconceived sense of how the manifestation must be.

You are allowing room for the best to enter your life.

You affirm God.

You affirm your trust in God.

You allow the highest and best.

Consider a life lived in Grace, using your words, and thoughts always in Grace. When you are seeking a job or a mate or an answer to a need, say out loud, "I wish it under Grace. I want it under Grace."

- Grace eliminates the old laws.

- Grace lifts us to God.

- Your words become blessings to you and those around you.

- Grace helps you to release yourself to your higher Source.

- You are no longer confined to what works on this earthly level.

Choose Your Highest Good

Choose whatever it is that is for your higher good. If you don't know what this is, ASK!

ASK YOURSELF...ASK THE ANGELS...ASK GOD...ASK YOUR SOURCE...ASK NATURE...ASK THE UNIVERSE.

Tell them to let you know.

Tell them you are willing to know on a deeper and higher level.

Allow the higher powers to work for you rather than blocking them from your world.

Say out loud that you are *willing* to know what has been in your heart and proclaim your *willingness* to receive the information.

There is power in your words! Be *willing* to listen. Be *willing* to hear even if it seems illogical.

Be *willing* to act on information received. Don't wait for flawlessness and safety. There is no such thing really.

Be *willing* to believe in your intuition even if it may appear less than perfectly logical.

Consider the riches that started with a wish or desire.

Letting Go of the Negative

Paying attention to or dwelling on the negative harms you.

When you align yourself with negativity, anger, or sorrow, you deplete your positive energy. You start to build a wall by saying, "I refuse to participate with God, the Source." This refusal puts you in the arena of *cause and effect*.

If you find yourself there, don't surrender to it saying, "That's my karma." Instead say:

> CANCEL, CANCEL, CANCEL.
> ERASE, ERASE, ERASE.

Then restate your affirmations with great energy. Practice *Love, Praise, Gratitude and Appreciation*—and let go.

Saying this will allow you to feel good. Your good feeling allows you to look around with *new eyes*.

It's just like turning a light on—or the sun coming out on a cloudy day when you felt like things weren't going your way. Then suddenly the sun comes out, the wind comes, the sky is blue and you find yourself feeling powerful and strong. Anything that comes to you is going be very good and you will have a change in attitude—and that's what we all really want.

So practice. Practice *Love, Praise, Gratitude and Appreciation*!

Let go.

God makes a new way.

Letting Go Is Possible

Letting go of past and present resentments, fears, negativity, angers, and hatreds may seem to be impossible.

Letting go may seem like an uphill battle, a daunting task.

START FROM WHERE YOU ARE.

Discover where you are no matter how awful it might seem. Be present with yourself... Allow yourself to feel.

These negative feelings may have been a part of you for so long that you fear being left with emptiness.

As you let go, please know that living and going forth in *Love, Praise, Gratitude and Appreciation* fills you with nourishment. Remember the love exercise? Fill the parts that may seem empty with love and light. Please remember you are never alone!

The emptiness is replaced with positive feelings.

As you start on your journey of change—bringing with you the tools of *Love, Praise, Gratitude and Appreciation*—you *realize* that certain restrictive feelings inside lift and go away.

IT WILL HAPPEN.

As you cease to feel resentment or fear and you start operating out of a place of *Love, Praise, Gratitude and Appreciation*, there will be a visible change in the way others respond to you.

PLEASE KNOW THIS!

Health

As you put your attention to what is right and positive in your life—giving thanks and praise for those blessings, *no matter how small*—you find that healing is occurring on many levels.

You already know that you may use your imagination to help you feel more vigorous, healthy, robust, creative, and peaceful. The addition of living a life filled with *Love, Praise, Gratitude, and Appreciation* magnifies the sense of well-being and health.

> Focusing on *Love, Praise, Gratitude, and Appreciation*
> brings EASE into your life and releases DIS-EASE.

GIVING THANKS AND PRAISE
ACTUALLY CHANGES THE CHEMISTRY OF THE BRAIN.

This is very important to *realize*. You can take charge of your chemistry through letting go with *Love, Praise, Gratitude, and Appreciation*.

You know that imagination is so powerful it creates new neural pathways and allows the serotonin—which is the "feel-good" chemical in your brain—to be more prevalent.

Please remember that *Love, Praise, Gratitude, and Appreciation* is also a very powerful tool for your health, happiness and well-being.

Emotional Effects

Living in fear, anger and resentment affects every organ, every cell in the body. The liver filters the poisons from the body, and anger is a poison.

On the physical level, drink water, breathe and sleep. Have good bowel movements. Eat the right foods for your body. You won't get as much from *Love, Praise, Gratitude, and Appreciation* if your body isn't healthy. If you are healthy, you will open the channels even more and in the ways that you want.

What is in your body? Are you holding a grudge? Do you have anger at the world? Even while holding this negativity, your wishes *may* get through this *filter of anger.* You may still manifest but perhaps not as abundantly as you wish.

Get rid of this negative to get to the abundance.

Bring the negative to the light.

Don't be afraid.

When you bring your negativity to God—to the light—it is exposed and then reduced or dissolved. It is left powerless and disintegrates into the nothingness from which it came—*misunderstanding.*

Words Have Power

Your words send out your desires to the Source. These words are energy and create a certain shape, feeling, vibration.

- Each word you speak has an effect.

- Each word you speak has power.

- Each word you speak goes forth with energy to the Source.

YOUR WORDS HAVE POWER. As you send your words forth for manifestation, know that you get back so much more than what you asked for.

As you do this work and have courage to ask and are willing to receive, you will see that each time you will receive *more*.

It takes courage to allow your words to go forward, and it takes a willingness to allow yourself to receive more and more.

The beauty of this process is that it builds on itself.

THE JOURNEY IS WORTH IT.

The Inner Child and LPGA

How you perceive and walk through the world today was developed and built in your childhood.

Perhaps when you were growing up certain people you loved did not keep their word, and you experienced a deep pain in your heart.

You may have been left feeling confused, angry, sad, and unloved.

YOU MAY HAVE SET UP DEFENSES
THAT YOU STILL USE TODAY.

As an adult, you have the capability of going back and understanding what the child's mind could not.

You are actually able to heal the child parts of yourself
by letting those parts know that the child is now *safe*.

You, *the conscious you,* is now okay.

You can let the parts know that you can and will
love them unconditionally.

NAME THOSE PARTS BLAMELESS.

As an adult, you reconnect with your child, your innocence.

You may now erase the misunderstandings, and erase the adulterations that you accepted, which have nothing to do with you.

You may choose to forgive, start fresh, and walk in GRACE.

FORGIVING will help you be responsive to what is in your life today, so that you may go forth with a deeper clarity in *Love, Praise, Gratitude, and Appreciation.*

Seek what is for your highest good.

For it is in living and being open
to embracing the wishes of your heart and soul
that you receive a new zest for life.

Appreciate Your Day

Please become adept at looking for
what you can appreciate in your day.

Give thanks and praise
for what you already have!

Use both imagination and discernment
to create and manifest
what is for your highest good.

Give love and thanks for the changes.

Things will change
for the better
in your world daily.

REMEMBER...

• *Each day make a decision to be pleasant,* to have an ATTITUDE OF GRATITUDE. Know that this attitude expands and opens the channels from you to the Source.

• *You will see there is always something new* and intriguing right before you.

• *You will begin to appreciate* how infinitely faceted God is. When you ask in *Love, Praise, Gratitude, and Appreciation*—and send it forth—what you receive back will be infinitely more than what you asked for.

• *You have expanded as a human being* in your ability to love. Have patience in your ability to see and understand.

• *You will be given opportunities* to meet wonderful people around the globe.

• *You will be able to dissolve your personal issues* in ways that are magical and lovely—in ways that would have seemed impossible in earlier years.

Your happiness is NOW an everyday experience.

Changing Your World with
LPGA: ACTIVITIES

Going forth in *Love, Praise, Gratitude, and Appreciation* presents changes in your world so that you are living each day of your life with a rich fullness.

1. As you now know, imagination and discernment play key roles in the choices you make every day.

    So begin by taking a situation—an event—a quality of your being and apply *Love, Praise, Gratitude, and Appreciation* to it.

    Have you noticed any change? Do this every day for a week, then revisit your answer.

    _____

    _____

    _____

    _____

    _____

    _____

2. Come down into your solar plexus and say, "I salute you, child, with *Love, Praise, Gratitude, and Appreciation* and blessings of God. I am willing to receive you now."

   Take a moment to breathe, and allow your mind to be open. Write down your body feelings, sensations, perceptions, intuitions.

   Remember, if you get scared, don't worry, just breathe into the *fear*.

   Repeat your affirmation.

   _____

   _____

   _____

   _____

   _____

   _____

   Remember that *fear* has information to give you.

   Make friends with your *fear*.

3. Write down ten things that you love.

_____

_____

_____

_____

_____

Write down ten things that you can give praise for or praise to in your life.

_____

_____

_____

_____

_____

Write down ten things that you have gratitude for.

_____

_____

_____

_____

_____

Write down ten things that you can have appreciation for in your life.

_____

_____

_____

_____

_____

Now, after writing all those things down, I invite you to make your own affirmations from your words of *Love, Praise, Gratitude, and Appreciation.* See what happens. Experience where your mind goes.

4. Take a challenging situation. How could you apply *Love, Praise, Gratitude, and Appreciation to* this situation?

Using your discernment, what is it within that may be a block to your applying these new principles?

How has this block served you in the past?

To dissolve the block, apply the principles. What skills do you now have that make the block unnecessary?

Once you have this knowledge, allow *Love, Praise, Gratitude, and Appreciation* to be present and flow. Please write down your thoughts.

5. Think of what you would like to happen in the next year.

   Use the skills you have gained in Imagination, Discernment, and, now, in *Love, Praise, Gratitude, and Appreciation* to bring color and perspective to your desires.

   Use discernment for what is true for you now in this moment.

   Apply Love to that—then apply Praise—then Gratitude—then Appreciation. Using this exercise, what paths have revealed themselves to you?

Changing Your World with
LPGA: AFFIRMATIONS

*I give gratitude and praise
for all that lies before me this day.*

*I live with wonder at what is before me
and I am grateful.*

*I look with love upon myself and my world,
and my world becomes more loving.*

I give praise for all the blessings in my life.

*I am grateful for all the goodness I have right now:
my health, my happiness, my peace of mind.*

Goodness brings positive, loving, and graceful
changes into my world.

As I am willing to love,
my world is willing to change
as I am willing to love.

I dissolve all that is not meant for me right now.

I am open and receptive to the great love within me,
and I send it forth, dissolving all that is not mine today.

My world opens with the great love
that I send forth through my heart.

My world now changes under Grace,
and all good and loving growth is mine today.

Your Own Affirmations:
JOURNAL

Your Own Affirmations:
JOURNAL

Changing Your World with
LPGA: MEDITATIONS

PLEASE GET COMFORTABLE. Breathing down to your belly, take your attention inside, allowing the soft part of your abdomen to go in and out with each long, slow breath.

Follow your breath. Allow each breath to take you deeper.

Become aware of what you are feeling in this moment. Become aware of your thoughts, feelings, ideas, and structures which are normally silent during your day-to-day activities. Observe without evaluation or judgment. Be present and allow the best of all possibilities.

Employing your senses of sight, touch, smell, taste, and hearing, use the following suggestions as a way to focus your attention.

When you are finished with your meditation, please write down your perceptions.

1. This section is about changing your mind by having thoughts of *Love, Praise, Gratitude, and Appreciation.*

   Become aware of your mind chatter. I would like you to just start saying to yourself, "Love, love, love." Say it about a hundred times and notice the difference. There tends to be a lightness. Write down how you now feel.

2. Truth and love may be thought of as the building blocks of the very cells of your being.

    Concentrate on the positives in your life.

    Focus only on the gifts you have. Pick one, two, or three on which to focus. Give praise for those gifts. Write down what you sense, feel, and intuit.

3. The words, "thank you," are a very *powerful* affirmation. These words acknowledge, and these words give praise.

    Relax into your mediation with the words, "thank you."

    See them, hear them, feel them. Write down your thoughts, insights and feelings.

REMEMBER, LIVING A LIFE

IN WHICH LOVE, PRAISE, GRATITUDE,

AND APPRECIATION ARE CENTRAL

ALLOWS YOU TO CONNECT

WITH YOUR HIGHER SOURCE

ON A LEVEL THAT IS NOT POSSIBLE

IN ANY OTHER WAY.

Changing Your World with
LPGA: GUIDED IMAGERY

PLEASE TAKE A MOMENT, get comfortable, breathe and allow your mind to expand. Allow yourself to go into places where you have never been. It takes work to expand your consciousness—to begin to lengthen those times of insight and bliss—so that you may begin to *believe* the messages that reside there for you.

1. Journey into your heart. Choose one of your heart's desires or dreams. If you have problems doing this, ask which one would like to come out.

   Take a mental journey, giving thanks and praise, as you see your world changing.

2. Are you currently in a situation where you don't feel *Love, Praise, Gratitude or Appreciation* as part of your everyday life? If so, look deeply and think about the love of an animal, an appreciation for the flowers around you, or a memory of a loving person. Replace the feelings in the unpleasant situation with these. Be one with the positive thoughts. How are you now feeling?

_____

_____

_____

_____

_____

_____

_____

_____

_____

_____

_____

_____

_____

_____

_____

_____

_____

_____

_____

_____

3. Go to a time when someone, a family member, a friend, or a stranger praised you for something you did. It could be as small as picking up a piece of litter from the street or as large as saving someone's life. Go to that time, look around. Pay attention to what you see, feel, and hear. Remember the voice of praise that was given to you and allow it to be felt by you right now. Bring that into your heart. Allow yourself to give praise to you and for you. Bask in it. Remember you are wonderful right now. Go forward in your journey.

Changing Your World with LPGA:
JOURNAL

Changing Your World with LPGA:
JOURNAL

Manifesting Your Wishes, Dreams, and Desires

The dreams of your heart
are in reality
the heavenly blueprints
for your life.

Manifesting

TO MANIFEST IS TO HAVE something become apparent to the senses so that it may be made clear and evident.

The lesson on *Manifesting Your Wishes, Dreams, and Desires* will help you make your heart's passion a reality. In this chapter, you will discover how manifesting one's wishes is a miraculous gift to us from the universe, from our Source.

The steps to manifesting your wishes, dreams, and desires are straightforward. But before we begin, I want you now to take a moment and review all that you have accomplished when you began to practice the principles shared with you in Lessons One, Two, and Three.

In this lesson, our fourth lesson, you are going to use all your newly developed or expanded skills and senses to activate the dreams from your imagination and allow yourself to amplify your heart's desire.

So please—

Take a moment and reflect on the opportunities that you have seen appear when you activated your *Imagination* and brought your focus to those ideas which captured your interest and brought you joy.

Take a moment and reflect on your newly expanded sense of knowing that you gained when you developed your skills of *Discernment*.

Take a moment and reflect on the positive experiences in your life, which have multiplied as you have lived your life in *Love, Praise, Gratitude, and Appreciation.*

How are you now and what are your feelings?

Jot down a few notes.

_____

_____

_____

_____

_____

_____

_____

_____

_____

_____

_____

_____

_____

_____

_____

_____

_____

_____

_____

_____

_____

_____

_____

_____

_____

_____

_____

Sweetness and Goodness Are Yours

Manifesting Your Wishes, Dreams, and Desires is about selecting those activities, objects, thoughts, actions, and ideas that your discernment informs you will foster the achievement of your highest good.

I WANT YOU TO REMEMBER
BY VIRTUE OF YOUR VERY EXISTENCE
YOU ARE ENTITLED TO RECEIVE
SWEETNESS AND GOODNESS.

I want you to internalize—that because you are you—you are entitled to a sweetness and goodness which includes love, joy, happiness, and material prosperity.

As you have been living your life in *Love, Praise, Gratitude, and Appreciation,* have you realized the many gifts and riches that are already in your life?

KNOW

*Love, joy, happiness, and material prosperity
are in your divine plan.*

*They are at this very moment,
in the universal bank waiting for you.*

Building on the earlier lessons,
you will learn that what you
send forth into the universe with faith
will be returned to you
with a greatness unforeseen.

Manifesting Is—

- ABOUT bringing into being, in a material way, what you desire.

- ABOUT bringing into being something that has energy, a presence, that can be sensed with the five physical senses.

- ABOUT taking something that is on the plane of ideas and bringing it into the plane of the physical world.

- ABOUT bringing into your being new senses, including a sense of well being, a sense of peacefulness, a sense of understanding, a sense of contentment, a sense of wonder, a sense of joy and developing new senses which enrich your very existence.

This lesson is about presenting ideas, presenting ways that work, that are proven methods to bring into the physical realm what is for your highest good.

The Power of the Spoken Word

Let's start with the power in the spoken word because part of the process of manifesting is being conscious of what you are putting out into the universe verbally.

> *How many of us damn everything,*
> *including God, on a regular basis,*
> *then turn around and*
> *wonder why things aren't going right?*

You know that words, your conveyed thoughts, have the power to hurt and the power to heal. You have spoken from anger and you have spoken from love. You also know that words have the power to affirm or negate, to create and tear down.

> *Know that the spoken word has power.*

> *Know that once something is said, it is said.*

Words, once spoken, are difficult to change or erase. Many of us have at one time or another said something that we wish we could take back. We might have spoken out of frustration or maybe we were physically tired. You know that these words and their effects lingered.

WORDS HAVE POWER.

Now expand on this knowledge and consider that everything you say happens to you first. Take a moment now to let this sink in:

EVERYTHING YOU SAY
HAPPENS TO YOU FIRST.

Consider, before you have uttered a word,
that your mind had to select that specific word.

Your mind had to place that word in the sentence,
and your mind had to fit that word into the bigger idea
that you were conveying.

Choosing the word placed you in the position of
the developer, the perceiver, and the speaker.

Once something is said,
it has been sent out into the universe.

Remember that it is your *throat chakra* that sends out the wishes, dreams and desires to the Source, so that the Source may then return them to you manifested.

Scientists now tell us that all reality is made up of various *frequencies*— a confirmation of how powerful your words really are.

> *Your voice and your words are frequencies*
> *and vibrations sent out into the universe.*

Picture the vibrations of your words
as pebbles cast into a pool of water
that send out ripples across the pool.

Your words create ripples in the universe
and are a significant factor in what the
Source—the Universe—returns to you.

In essence, your words act as a magnet
drawing to you what you desire in your heart.

WHAT ARE YOUR WORDS
ATTRACTING INTO YOUR LIFE?

Please take a moment and reflect on the words that are threaded throughout your daily speech.

- Are you speaking words originating from fear, frustration, bitterness, negativity, or anger?

- Are you speaking words of scarcity or of want?

- Are your words critical of those around you?

- Are your words harsh?

To effect change in your life and manifest what is for your highest good requires you to begin speaking words of peace and abundance.

Take a moment to think of these words and write them down.

Attract Your Highest Good

To attract what is for your highest good requires you to pay attention to your words. Earlier, when you started living your life in *Love, Praise, Gratitude, and Appreciation*, you began to experience an expanded sense of life's possibilities.

You have already noticed that the more you acknowledged and gave praise and gratitude for your blessings, the more blessings came your way! The more you showed love and appreciation, the more love and appreciation appeared in your life!

Speak Your Truth In Words

As you speak, you magnify in words your feelings and thoughts.

With words, you are the speaker of your own Truths.

- If you want to lose weight, do not continue to state how fat you are, for your fatness will continue to be magnified. Instead speak words of health and fitness for that is what will grow in your life.

- If you want to be in a healthy loving relationship, do not continue to speak words of how terrible men or women are and how they are no good. Instead talk about how much you enjoy people and how stimulating they are.

- Instead of continuing to talk about how broke you are, begin to focus your attention on the abundance in your life.

- Always be conscious of your words, even when you are the customer. When dealing with a salesperson, thank that person. Tell them to have a good day. Appreciate their efforts. This will put into the universe appreciation for labor.

  You benefit from the appreciation you give to others.

From the Heart

As significant as the power of the spoken word is, it must come from the heart. You know, it is your heart which pumps your life force through your body.

Know now, it is your heart, your soul, which is the body's meeting place of heaven and earth.

The spoken word then needs to come from your heart.

It is the translator of the human brain to the universe.

Your heart is key to turning limited into unlimited. Everyone has heard the saying that a person has HEART to indicate dedication to a goal, a striving to achieve.

This, though, is only part of the power emanating from your heart.

It is your heart, the language of your heart,
your heart's intentions—that is the language of the universe.

YOUR HEART
IS YOUR CONNECTION
TO UNIVERSAL LOVE,
TO UNIVERSAL LIGHT,
TO UNIVERSAL TRUTH.

When you speak words from your heart,
your whole being resonates with your heart's power.

It is through the attainment
of what you desire from your heart,
that you are reconnecting your outer self
with your inner self, with your Source.

You are accessing your core—
free from filters, free from teachings
that you have internalized as Truth—
so that you are no longer aware that
you view life through a lens or filter.

Filters

Life has a way of layering filters within you that set the self at odds in ways that can be difficult to detect. You now must become aware of the filters that are between you and seeing clearly, because filters lock you into a rigid mold, halting the perfect manifestation of your dreams.

- Filters, such as socio-economic standing, education, teachings, and societal norms, act as barriers to your being able to attract and to manifest.

- There are filters of teachings which state that you should not ask for help and that what you attain is only valuable if you attain "it" without assistance.

- Filters, which instruct that you be satisfied with your *lot in life*, tell you that it is wrong to ask for more.

- Some filters teach you to feel guilty about what you have or want because others are "less fortunate."

- Still other filters trigger feelings of fear or guilt when you desire more or dream about having more in your life.

- And then there are filters which make you fall in line with societal norms as the only option.

Go inside and explore—

- Do you believe that it is okay to have dreams that go beyond what society, or your family, or your friends, dictate is acceptable for you?

- Do you believe that it is your lot in life to accept what you have been given?

- Are you afraid of success?

Please understand that filters of fear and guilt are filters between you and God, between you and your Source.

WHAT TEACHINGS, OR FILTERS, DO YOU HOLD AS TRUTH?

Take a moment to write down a few of the teachings you hold as Truths. *Where, when,* did you decide to make them true?

Awareness Is Key

Becoming aware of the filters in your life will assist you in developing an awareness of those things which have kept you from having your heart's desire manifest in your life.

> *Becoming aware of the filters which contain*
> *and restrain your dreams, wishes, and desires*
> *is crucial to manifesting your highest good.*

Perhaps you have been taught that being "selfless" is one of the highest spiritual goals that one may achieve. But to be selfless means you give up your "self," the self which is your gift from God.

> *To create, to grow a true self, is to nourish God,*
> *the Source, in a most honorable way.*
> *A true self is vital.*

In Truth, when you develop your gifts to their highest potential you are *gifting* to your creator a more developed *Self*. So, to achieve and obtain your heart's desire is a great *compliment* to God, the Source, for you have put into practice and action all that has been provided to you.

Please know, the fear or guilt that some people experience when asking for material things is misguided. When we obtain what is for our highest good, we are in essence returning to our *true* selves because the real Source lives within us,

always there
always present
always available

and always wanting to be expressed and manifested.

We are infinite.
In our Source, we are boundless and endless.

There is no such thing as finite within ourselves or within God.

Are you limiting yourself by trying to fit
into some finite definition or cause?

Overcome Guilt

If you experience feelings of guilt for wanting more than food on the table and a roof over your head, please know that when you manifest what you desire from your heart, you are glorifying the universe and opening doors for others to receive as well.

You are not making less for others,
rather you are forging a way
to make the impossible possible for others.

You are expanding what is in the world
for others to receive.

Please take a moment to internalize that:

AS YOU RECEIVE,
YOU CREATE ADDITIONAL SPACE
FOR OTHERS TO RECEIVE.

The world is only richer for God's children
to obtain what they desire.

God's Grace

Understand that our universe is as infinite as God's *power* and *love*.

God does not operate in scarcity.

Know then, that our Source is as unlimited as the universe.

Think about this... When I was a child, I loved to go to the beach. I believe it was then that I was told that there were more stars in the universe than grains of sand on all the beaches of the world. I now believe there are more galaxies in the universe than all the grains of sand in the entire world.

You do not need to live a life of scarcity.
You may live a life of opulence and peace.

It is God's desire that you receive your divinely chosen prosperity. Material abundance can be part of manifesting and giving back to God. However, material abundance does not take the place of the Source.

Always give the Source
praise and gratitude for each blessing received.

Always know that it is through God's Grace
that the power to manifest is in each one of us.

God Is Our Gift

God is the gift and the giver.

The gift can never be taken from me or you,
because God can never be taken from me or you.

It is only we who replace God with misguided ideas and therefore limit, through our filters, the Divine plan.

We need to go to our Source as **a first resort**—not only when things are falling apart. We need to tune in and listen to God.

Take a moment. Breathe and calm down.

- Become one with the universe God created.
- Join your presence with the Higher Source.
- Picture yourself as a drop of water in the ocean.

One drop of water left alone in the sun will evaporate; but as a drop of water in the ocean, you have the power to carve granite.

God is the ocean.

Through *Love, Praise, Gratitude, and Appreciation*—and now through learning how to manifest—you gain power to move the mountains in your life—to move doubt and fear and guilt—and allow that flow of love, prosperity, and abundance to be active in your life.

Be Willing to Take Care

As shared earlier, the steps to manifesting the wishes, dreams, and desires of your heart are straightforward.

Starting right now...

Take care with your words.
And with your words choose to speak
of abundance, peace, health, happiness,
prosperity, gratitude, praise, and appreciation.

Be joyful in your speech and in your receipt of the boundlessness of the Source.

In time, you will find that your life will no longer be controlled by physical laws—such as cause and effect—but rather by the higher spiritual law of Grace.

You will find...

...that you regularly go to God *first* for everything.

You have already learned that if you are willing to give *Love, Praise, Gratitude and Appreciation*, you will be willed Grace and abundance in every aspect of your life.

Consider...

> IF YOU ARE WILLING,
> YOU WILL BE WILLED
> ALL THAT YOU SEEK.

Please know...

> *There are openings*
> *in your physical universe*
> *where wonders occur.*

Just prepare to receive and continue to take action through thoughts, words, deeds, imagination, and discernment to realize your dreams.

> *Your life*
>
> *will start to become*
>
> *a magical place*
>
> *full of*
>
> *wonderment*
>
> *and joy.*

Beginning to Practice

When starting to put into practice the principles of this lesson—begin by believing that you *are* supposed to have what is from your heart's desire.

YOU ARE!

As you believe and take action on your beliefs, your *closet* will be getting cleaned.

The very act of creating new energy
and directing the flow of certain energy
dissolves blocks or filters.

It is important to feel the energy.

It is important to be heart-felt with enthusiasm.

Pay attention to your intuition and your creative ideas, work-arounds, and solutions.

Action is key.

Reflection is key.

Positive thoughts are key.

Please know...

Manifesting your wishes, dreams, and desires
is not about doing A-B-C in order to receive 1-2-3.

Manifesting your desires
is not a linear activity,
but rather it is a
multi-dimensional *practice*
calling on all your senses
as you operate under Universal Law.

Matter Has Changed

We have been taught that matter has three dimensions—length, width, and depth.

Yet as scientists continue to conduct research on matter, they find that matter is *not* limited to length, width, and depth.

Scientists are finding that on the deeper levels...

> *There are no limitations.*
> *Indeed, there are unlimited possibilities.*

To provide you with a mental picture, think of one single atom as being on the fifty-yard-line of a football field. The electron of this one single atom reaches clear past the goal posts and way into the end zone.

> *There is space within matter,*
> *and where there is space,*
> *there is opportunity.*

This is magic, and it brings with it a sense of mastery. It facilitates your letting go of control and believing, trusting, and acting according to your intuition.

YOU ARE NOW
IN CHARGE
OF YOUR OWN LIFE.

If you believe and let go,
a new control and mastery results.

Sounds paradoxical? Being a human being is being a paradox. Know that the principles, which begin to open those hidden doors within your world, are within you.

Go inside your heart, stay present. In your heart is the intuition to understand what you need to do next. Know, *know*, that anything is possible.

Realize there is more for you.
Realize you create your own limits.
Look for options.

*Know
what it is
that is
motivating
what you want.*

Know Your Intention

Why do you want that new car? Can it be a Chevy? Does it have to be a Lexus?

Allow all possibilities to come forward.

Use your discernment to see what will be your next step.

Don't settle.

Make it more real, giving your energy somewhere to focus.

Don't be deterred by others.

Keep going forward.

If you are looking for someone to marry with certain qualities, work on developing those qualities within yourself.

Like attracts like.

Going Inside

If you believe that you have taken all actions possible to obtain your wishes, dreams and desires, and you have been giving *Love, Praise, Gratitude, and Appreciation*—but you do not see the manifestation—then you need to go back *inside*.

When you go inside...

Use your discernment to see if what you set out to obtain is really something for which you have an immediate need or desire.

Ask yourself why is it that you want this?

- Now use your imagination to visualize what your current life would be like with your desires manifested—add color and texture.

- Think back on what you thought you wanted and then later realized you were better off not having.

- Make room within yourself where wishes, dreams, and desires can manifest. If you realize this is deeply what you want—then focus.

- Reignite your passion.

- Feel and know that goodness is there for you.

Please begin to understand what it is that truly will bring about your highest good.

Steps to Manifesting

Know that there are steps to manifesting, so that what you desire can take a presence in your life right now.

It is not something that requires you to somehow be perfect—or somehow think—or do something to be worthy. You do not have to have your life in perfect order to begin.

Simply begin from where you are.

Let me now share with you the principles, and then lead you through them step by step.

STEP ONE

Sit down and write down as succinctly as you can a story of what you desire.

(The more clearly you can imagine what you want, the more clearly you can write down what you want.)

Explain, be descriptive—use color, motion, sound, and scents in your story.

You will know you are on the right track if you begin to feel either a sense of *calm* or a sense of *joy*.

Sometimes there is a sense of overwhelm which means that something has come up for you to look at.

Any panicky feelings do not mean that you shouldn't have what you want. They may mean that you need to look at your filters.

Continue to put your thoughts and passion toward manifesting what you desire.

Know that on many levels you are allowing the channels of manifestation to open their gates to you.

You will get stronger and stronger.

Solutions will appear as your imagination creates new avenues and ways of receiving.

Trust is vital to manifestation.

You must trust yourself.

Trust that what

comes from your heart,

from the Source,

is good and viable for you

STEP TWO

Take action according to your intuition, for intuition is God's inspiration in and through you.

It is in having and nourishing this trust that you will be able to step out and in to *faith*.

> *Trust and faith*
> *bring to you an ability to recognize*
> *those actions and sensations*
> *key to attaining your heart's desires.*

Know that it takes courage to open channels within your *self* to receive.

Take time to develop the courage to dissolve inner resistance which may be a result of filters, fear, or guilt.

> *Let go of those*
> *three-dimensional barriers*
> *which keep you from attaining*
> *what is for your highest good.*

Move on, remembering always that...

All things are possible in God.

Practicing the above will open the way for what you desire to manifest in your present day reality.

Question your true intentions to set your determination mentally upon the action or result.

STEP THREE

Pay attention to what you have developed using the true guide inside of you.

This guide is showing you the way to manifestation of your wishes, dreams and desires. Once you change your reactions, or once you move into a different place, then your circumstances will not stay the same.

Sometimes when you are on the road to manifesting what you want—and it appears that nothing is moving—go back and take a look inside at any filters still existing which are blocking the manifestation.

Say out loud:
ERASE, CANCEL.

Cancel in threes:
CANCEL, CANCEL, CANCEL.

And then state:
ERASE, ERASE, ERASE.

Three is the number of creation and creativity.

THREE IS THE MOST POWERFUL OF TOOLS.

The first is to breathe!

It is to inhale spirit and God into the body!

The second is water!

To bring in spirit in water cleanses and heals
and cools downs and brings the flow.

The third is sleep!

In sleep we demonstrate our trust and faith in God
as we allow our spirit to go to God to heal us
and to refresh and renew our bodies.

Before you go to sleep, think of whatever it is
that makes you feel very happy,
and send this happiness up to heaven.

*Your last words and thoughts should be thoughts and words
of gratitude offered up to God for the blessings in your life.*

These actions will allow your unconscious mind better access
to the Source for better sleep and easier ability to manifest.

STEP FOUR

Four is the number of sealing. Say it three times to cancel and four times to seal.

This is important.

If you find you have absorbed the filter of someone else, it is now okay to give that energy up to God for cleansing and purification. It is just a mistaken idea.

For example, you may want to find a better paying job or a job that offers additional challenges; however, you have been searching and you can't find what you want.

Go inside and see if there is another filter which may need to be addressed.

This filter may be yours or it may not be yours. You may have absorbed the filter of someone close to you. You may have absorbed the filter for someone else.

Inside, do you feel that you do not have the skills to perform at another job? Have you been told and so believe that you will not amount to anything greater than you are now?

Dissolve Your Filters

Start to dissolve these filters. Know that they are not true. You are God's child. You are perfect and already whole. In Greek the word perfect means "already whole."

Work on your affirmations. Then take steps. Perhaps enroll in a class to get more knowledge. Get three-dimensional validation.

If your desire is not manifesting, then it is time to go back to God.

Ask God, the Source, that you be more inspired. Let the Source know that you are willing to receive new inspiration—new ideas—regarding this situation.

Be willing to change the way you act in the three-dimensional world.

Be willing to do things in an unusual way.

Be willing to be creative.

Be willing to go inside and discern where you are at the present moment.

STEP FIVE

Use your imagination to expand your desires.

Write them down. The first sentence should be short and affirmative. The second sentence is more descriptive—accessing your senses regarding what you want, what you feel, and how you want to be treated.

Describe what it is you wish to have in your life. As you use all your senses and your imagination, you start putting forth *commands on the universe* to make so what it is you are saying.

The more of your five senses that you use,
the more powerful your command is
—and will be heard as such—
from the universe.

STEP SIX

Now go inside and access the discernment ability that you learned previously.

- Listen to your intuition and to your senses.

- *Allow yourself to dream,* and pay attention to those dreams.

- Allow yourself to be what others may consider *illogical.*

- Live by and through your intuition!

- *Follow your intuition*—your hunches—fully, wholeheartedly.

Don't be concerned if at first you run into a roadblock. This is a natural part of manifesting.

Sometimes roadblocks can be seen as a sign that a pause is needed.

Sometimes the pause may be about taking another route, asking for something else, or asking for something different.

Sometimes the roadblock is a sign that a filter has been activated. In this case, it is important to stay with the filter, to let it come into consciousness.

If the block seems too large, be willing to consult others who have experience and ability to help dissolve the block.

STEP SEVEN

Please remember to put yourself in what you want manifested as if it has already occurred.

For example, if you want to manifest a new car, smell the interior, hear the engine, see the shiny color, speak the words of ownership, go out and get a driver's license, call for insurance rates, go sit in the type of car you want.

- Imagine and ask that all happens *under Grace* in the best possible way, in a divinely chosen way, which only offers good and harms no one.

- Join with what you want. If you are always bad-mouthing rich people, chances are you won't be able to be rich.

- Join with what you want. Watch your words. Be positive. Be affirmative. (Go to the dealership—test drive the car.)

Please go to your intuition and ask, "What is my next step?" Be willing to follow your hunches and your inner thoughts.

Know that the universe has already heard your wishes and desires and is already moving toward their fulfillment.

Please continue this activity. It is not a one-time thing. Continue to do this step-by-step.

This is a fun adventure with a glorious outcome.

STEP EIGHT

Do It In A Grateful Way.

As well as visualizing the car, or whatever you want, tell the angels, *Thank You*!

Allow yourself to be able to receive in magical ways.

Use your imagination, your intuition, your inner guidance to reach out in ways that may not always be logical.

BE OPEN.

KNOW YOU DESERVE IT!

MANIFESTATION IN YOUR LIFE
CAN HAPPEN IN A
MIRACULOUS NUMBER OF WAYS.

The Steps Are Fluid

The above steps are not rigid. A sense of well-being and connectedness with the world around you is part of the process of manifesting.

It is not required that you conceive it as a wish first or as a dream first.

You make wishes from desires.

You see something that you like and you have a sense of yearning or longing to receive it. Then you embellish it with all your senses and energy, so that it becomes a kind of dream.

It becomes a yearning that is filled out, or colored in, or expanded. And it becomes expanded in a dream.

As you dream, you fill that dream with a kind of longing, and it becomes a wish, and you send the wish forth to God.

Stay positive.

Stay affirmative.

There are already abundant riches and wonders set aside for you. Allow these riches to occur.

Watch your words.

HAVE GOOD INTENTIONS
AND EXPECT TO RECEIVE!

Allow the Process to Occur

Allow your wish to expand. Be patient. Don't get into an attitude where you might feel, "If I can't have what I want, I'll have whatever I can get." This diminishes the workings of both the Source and your inner being. When you do this, you are actually going against yourself because your heart's desire is where you need to focus.

The problem is with your own belief system. Maybe you are thinking that obstacles are symbols or signs which are stating that your heart's desire is not for you.

Come back to your heart and ask, "Is this really a desire from my heart, or could this be something that I have been told to want?" *It is important to discern the difference.*

It Is Okay to Have Wants

It is okay to want material things.

We are in a material form. It is the greatest pleasure of the Source to lavish us abundantly with what we desire. If, however, you want something to get *one up on the Joneses,* that is not a *heart's desire.* That is a negative ego need—which means you are coming from weakness and not strength.

You can still manifest getting *one up on the Joneses* if you put your effort into it, but this is a very expensive manifestation.

It diminishes your core, because it is an *untruth.*

It is using your energy to support a lie.

And the lie is that getting *one up on the Joneses* will make you healthier, happier, give you more self-confidence, etc.

If you want a bigger house for your own pleasure—good.

If you want a bigger house just because you want something bigger than your neighbor, that's not good.

If what you are attracting into your life seems to be taking too long, take a deep breath and remind yourself that God wants you to have what is your Highest Good. Go within and ask yourself:

Am I doing all that I can do to
bring about my Highest Good?

Are my steps taken with integrity?

Remember, your journey is taken one step at a time. If more steps are needed to manifest, then *know* that each step has a purpose and is *good.*

Each step taken brings you closer to your dream.

Be grateful for each step.

BIG DREAMS ARE VITAL...
...and may require more steps.

Bring in *Love, Praise, Gratitude, and Appreciation* as you are taking each step. Keep your eyes on the goal and be willing to allow and receive, continuing to ask if there is anything else you need to do to bring your dreams into manifestation in your life.

Use your discernment.

Stay positive.

Use your affirmations.

PLEASE ALLOW WHATEVER COMES
FROM YOUR INNER SELF TO BE VALID!

This is vital to growth.

Explore, contribute, participate,
and know that your inner self is safe.

Let all that is within you come forth
without judgment or the need to evaluate.

Allow what is within you to come forward
and be part of the experience.

Let your inner innocence be
present, heard, and activated!

Manifesting Your Wishes, Dreams, and Desires:
THE LESSONS

A Reminder

Sometimes when we look at the back of the jewel, we only see the dirty rock from which it grew, and we become so dejected and disheartened that we turn away with a confirmation of our worst fears.

I am now inviting you to look at the jewel from many *different* angles.

When you come upon the back of the jewel—the dirty rock—do not take that as anything other than a confirmation that growth of something wonderful has occurred.

Know that...
by changing your position
and going to the front,
you will receive the gifts
of the facets of the jewel.

The Lessons

1. TAKE A MOMENT TO GO INSIDE.

   Be willing to allow yourself to seek that jewel deep inside. Stop for a moment and be willing to breathe through your whole body—beginning with your head and all the way down to your toes. Pay attention to those places where there are good feelings, and allow those areas of stuckness to dissolve with your breath. Begin to contact those deep areas of well-being, and allow them to reveal to you what it is they truly desire. You are now on the path to discovering the personal jewels of your dreams, wishes and desires. Take a moment and write down what you have discovered. What is it that you desire?

2. ALLOW WHAT IS DESIRED TO BE LARGER.

Open additional dimensions to see what you desire, wish, dream, manifest in your life.

Use the skills you have already practiced. Having activated your imagination to open the door to all possibilities, you now use your skills of discernment to arrive at your heart's deepest desires.

You are ready to receive your wishes in a three-dimensional form.

What *are* your dreams, wishes and desires?

3. BELIEVE THAT WHAT YOU DESIRE HAS COME INTO A PHYSICAL FORM.

Act *as if*.

Act as if it has already come to you.

Take a breath, and with your imagination, let your sensations and perceptions and your five senses bloom—feeling what it feels like to have achieved that goal. Let yourself relish in your achievement of manifesting what your heart has desired. You have already done it. Let yourself feel it.

What would you do? What would you think? What would you tell your friends? What would you tell yourself? How would you act?

Manifesting Your Wishes, Dreams, and Desires: AFFIRMATIONS

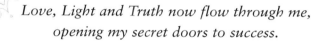

Love, Light and Truth now flow through me,
opening my secret doors to success.

The great Love of my heart shines forth
opening all good possibilities of my life to me now.

I am grateful for all that is mine at this moment in time
and all blessings light new possibilities on my path.

I give thanks and praise for all that is mine, knowing
that God has more in store for me in every moment that is.

I go forth in praise of all that is before me,
alighting anew my world with infinite blessings.

I give thanks that I am now open to the rich fullness
to embracing the wishes of my heart and soul,
bringing a new rich fullness to all
that I am and all that I will be.

With every breath I take I am reminded
of the miracles that are happening right now.

They are happening right now,
they are happening constantly.

I see my true self and all that I desire
now manifesting easily under Grace in a perfect way.

I am seeing all that is,
I am seeing all the channels that are mine open to me now.
I am able to know right now which path to follow.
I follow my golden path of enlightenment
that cuts its way through the desert into my oasis.

The great love of my heart streams forth
opening all good possibilities for my life.
All that I desire is now manifested
under Grace in a perfect way.
The dreams of my heart go forth and
are manifested with love, Grace and wonder.

I now see that what I desire is
already present in my life in a wonderful way.
I give thanks for what I desire and require
and it is made manifest under Grace easily to me.

Your Own Affirmations:
JOURNAL

Your Own Affirmations:
JOURNAL

Manifesting Your Wishes, Dreams, and Desires: MEDITATIONS

1. FIND SOMETHING THAT YOU DESIRE or appreciate. Now allow that something to come very close to you and allow yourself to join with it though your breath.

   Let's take this desire, and join it with LOVE.

   Allow LOVE to be your guide in your search
   and on your journey of
   Love, Praise, Gratitude, and Appreciation.

   It's a journey into a land of wondrous feelings and thoughts—a journey where you see beauty, and you feel beauty, and you begin to have a deeper sense of well-being, of peace, of happiness.

2. As you embrace this flower, this animal, this person that you love, allow yourself to feel gratitude for this experience. Allow yourself to appreciate now the way you feel in all of your body and being about having this loving experience. Allow yourself to express that gratitude in statements of praise.

3. Close your eyes. Go down into the deepest part of your heart. What is the first desire that greets you? Allow it to appear completely before you. See it shining. See it full of energy. See it multi-colored. Allow it to manifest with Grace.

    Now, take a deep breath.

    Say, "Thank You."

    _____

    _____

    _____

    _____

    _____

    _____

    _____

    _____

    _____

    _____

    _____

    _____

    _____

    _____

    _____

    _____

4. Close your eyes. Go deep inside and allow your body to travel into the future. Allow the great light of the Source to permeate every cell in your body. Where are you? Who are you? Who is with you? What does it look like, feel like, taste like? What else do you notice?

Manifesting Your Wishes, Dreams, and Desires:
GUIDED IMAGERY

1. PICK A WISH.

What is your wish?

How could you make your wish grow in color or texture, in size or material?

How could you then allow your wish to go out into the universe?

Can you release it? Picture yourself releasing.

Give thanks for what is happening now.

Thank the angels. Thank the Source. Thank God.

Be willing to accept with gratitude, Grace and joy.

2. Go to what you desire—your dream.

    Visualize it. Embellish it with color, texture, size, and love.
    Imagine that it is already there for you.

    Now allow your wish to come into your heart.

    Go to your discernment.

    Ask your discernment: *Is there anything else that I need to
    do, feel, see or say to make this so in my life—right now—
    in a wonderful way, in a graceful way?*

    Listen. Be receptive.

    See yourself taking these steps.

3. Picture yourself living a dream. Go deeply inside. Really allow that sense of happiness.

   How are you feeling?

   What are you doing?

   Who are you?

   What are you wearing?

   How are you affected?

   Are there other people who make up that dream?

   What are they doing?

   What has changed?

   Come back inside.

4. Imagine that you are walking on a very peaceful beach. The breeze is blowing. The aroma of the ocean is inviting. You decide to sit down and allow your feet to touch the cool water. As you do, you send your deepest wishes into the ocean. As the waves gently return, they reveal to you the manifestation of your dreams. Allow each wave its gentle revelation in your journey.

Final Thoughts

As you reach the end of your journey in this book, I invite you to return again and again to the places of LOVE and PEACE on these pages.

Take this book with you wherever you go. Use it. When you need it, go to it. It is written for you.

Please remember that there is more LOVE for you than you could ever know, and always reach out to embrace yourself with this great LOVE.

The paths that you will take in your life will be many, and always remember that you are not alone.

Take the path of love,

and see all that is there for you,

all the kindness, all the support, all the new ideas,

all the things that tickle your fancy,

all the joyous gifts that

your angels and guides have for

YOU!

Manifesting Your Wishes, Dreams, & Desires:
JOURNAL

Manifesting Your Wishes, Dreams, & Desires:
JOURNAL

Acknowledgments

I WOULD LIKE TO THANK the following people who helped me make this book become manifest.

My many editors, Bill Ricardi, Kathleen Jason Moreau, Karen Sydney, Susan Winn, and proof reader, Sue Stanley.

Very special thanks and praise go to my wonderful book designer, who gladly doubled as an editor, support, and all-around good person, Dotti Albertine.

Thanks to illustrators Laura Schmidt and Frank Barcenas.

Very special thanks to my family and friends who stood by me through this process.

And, of course, all my love to our Source, God, the Angels, and Light Beings, for their inspiration, love and wisdom.

About the Author

CATHERINE ATHANS, Doctor of Clinical Psychology, is the author of several well-received books. She is a frequent guest lecturer on topics which enable people to improve the quality of their lives. The recipient of several humanitarian awards, she is the founder of the Morgan Manor Foundation. Morgan Manor donates to and supports the working poor in Santa Clara County, California. Dr. Athans wrote *Make Your Dreams Come True Now* to supplement her series of lectures entitled, *How to Manifest Your Wishes, Dreams, and Desires.*

In 2003, Dr. Athans was a delegate to the Global Peace Initiative for Women at the United Nations in Geneva, Switzerland. There she lectured on *How to Teach Children Peaceful Means of Communication.*

Dr. Catherine Athans is well-educated—scientifically, metaphysically, and intellectually. Her teachers—Dr. Meyer Friedman and Dr. Ray H. Rosenman—are, respectively, Director and Associate Director of the Harold Brunn Institute for Cardiovascular Research at Mount Zion Hospital and Medical Center in San Francisco. Both are internationally known cardiologists and the authors of hundreds of technical papers. Dr. Friedman is also the author of two medical textbooks, *Functional Cardiovascular Disease* and *Pathogenesis of Coronary Artery Disease.*

Dr. Athans is a protégé of the late Very Reverend Harold G. Plume—a world-renowned psychic surgeon, healer, and trans-medium. In addition, she worked closely with the Reverend and Healer Rosalyn Bruyere at the Healing Light Center Church in Los Angeles.

Catherine Athans also holds a doctorate of divinity. A trained scientist, Dr. Athans has contributed to Stanford University Center for Research in Disease Prevention, as well as SRI International Department of Behavioral Medicine.

www.angelsislandpress.com

www.angelsislandpress.com

www.angelsislandpress.com

www.angelsislandpress.com